FREE ADMISSION – ACCESS TO THE SOUL
POETRY AND SHORT STORIES

ISBN: 978-0-692-46341-3
LCCN: 1-1951175361

Copyright© 2014 by P.O.P Writers Guild

No part of this book may be reproduced or transmitted in any form or by any means electronic or mechanical, including photocopying, recording, or by any information storage and retrieval system, without permission in writing from the authors, except for the use of brief quotations in a book review.

Printed in the United States of America

PUBLISHED BY:
P.O.P Writers Guild
Senior Guild Master: Adrienne Bruce
Guild Master: Adrienne Bruce

Cover Concept: Jose Ortega
Cover execution by: The Graphic Art Department of
Jazzi Creations Publishing Service

BOOK LAYOUT & INTERIOR DESIGN BY:
Jazzi Creations Publishing Service
P.O. Box 490520
Chicago, Illinois 60649
Website: www.jazzicreations.com

EDITING TEAM:
Senior Editor: J.D Cooper
Copy Editor: Talia Lambarki
Beta Reader/Editor: R. Hale-Wallace,
Proofreader: Luverta Reames
Proofreader: Darnell Bruce

ART DESIGN TEAM:
Artist: Adrienne Bruce
Graphic Artist: JamieLynn Warber
Paper Artist: Valerie Winkfield
Photographer: Nate Cunningham of EnJay Photography
Guest Artist: Julie M. Holloway

In Memory of:
Kizzy Givens

KIZZY GIVENS 1977—2014

Free Admission:
Access to the Soul

POETRY & SHORT STORIES

P.O.P Writers Guild

Preamble, Overture & Prelude

Senior Guild Master
Adrienne Bruce

The P.O.P Writers Guild creates a judgment-free atmosphere which allows its writers to bare their souls and tear down walls that have trapped and restricted them from their flourishing futures.

On this journey of confessions, discoveries, and revelations, the writers take a stroll through their minds to uncover past pain, truths, and realities. These amazing people allow themselves to be taken out of their comfort zones to be pressed and squeezed, poked and prodded, peeled and revealed. Exposing failures, lies, mistakes and dirty little secrets that no one thought they would ever freely divulge.

The P.O.P writers give you free admission to access entry into the world of an amazing voyage into the depths of their souls. Each writer bares it all to identify with humanity, which enables them to open doors, break down barriers and bring light to life.

As you identify with them feel free to smile, laugh, or even cry. Relax and enjoy the rhythm of the storytelling that will engulf every fiber of your being.

The P.O.P Writers Guild has faced the loss of life of a member that have gracefully made its way back home. Kizzy Givens, one of our writers, has left her imprint forever etched in the crevices of our minds. She will live through the words that weave themselves throughout the pages of this publication. Fragments of Kizzy's life experiences and expressive writings will touch you deeply as you read and get to know her. For some of us, it has been a short acquaintance and for others a lifelong relationship. Sharing this opportunity has preserved Kizzy's life accomplishments, and her legacy is ours to remember forever.

THE DOORS TO THESE LIVES ARE NOW OPEN

"Writing is an exciting mind exercise, a workout that keeps your mental muscle, sharp while shaping your life."

—Adrienne Bruce

THE REVEAL
Adrienne Bruce
Guild Master

It is such a rush of joy and privilege to have written with such dedicated and committed writers. Completing *Free Admission Access to the Soul* was a challenge with all that life had presented.

This Guild has pressed their way! Knocked down obstacles and kept their composure. I am so honored to introduce to you prolific, profound poets and storytellers. Kateria Doty lead the guild as a gracious, generous host until the storm ripped her sail by the passing of her best friend whom indeed was a P.O.P Writer. The bond of the guild held her together until she could catch her breath.

Pamela Fagen took the guild by the horns and rallied the beautifully written poetic pieces and carefully constructed stories together to meet their extended deadline. Pam brings the seriousness of life to life. Poetically free to spit her lyrics, Kenya Renee was entertaining and real as she admitted the truth and held back nothing, not even embarrassing moments. Todd Parker kept everyone grounded with the male perspective. Todd, a perfect southern gentleman, who candidly kept his cool, the brother is deep! Jor'danna has a richness to her flow; it will engulf you as she peacefully and tranquilly delivers. Sharon Payne's feistiness will never keep you hanging, and she lets it rip, dumps it in your lap while you deal with it with your mouth wide open. You will meet Kizzy Givens as she fills your heart with love, reality, and laughter. The tribute to Kizzy will enlighten you to how many lives she effectively touched before her journey home.

Now, prop your pillows, pour your favorite drink, grab your quilt and give yourself permission to make new acquaintances.

Admit

1

I Cried Last Night

- **Clutter Free, Jor'Danna Davis** *10*
- **Lovely Lies, Sharon Payne** *12*
- **Descendants Pain, Kenya Renee** *15*
- **One Good Cry, Pamela S.B. Fagen** *18*
- **Reconnection To Reality, Katerria "Starr" Doty** *20*
- **Mama, Kizzy Givens** *22*
- **My People ◆ My Sins ◆ My Triumph, Todd Parker** *23*

CLUTTER FREE

It was a cold winter night, in the middle of December, and I was ambitiously preparing for a big move by getting rid of the clutter. As I cleaned and organized, I came across three big shoe boxes full of journals. My paternal grandmother introduced me to journal writing at the age of 9. She told me about the importance of having an outlet for feelings. I've always been the type that kept a lot of my own mess inside, and at the same time took in everyone else's clutter. So I'm talking 21 years of bottled up and misplaced emotions.

   I began to open the boxes and look through each journal one by one. My thoughts danced around in the sphere of my mind, and a lump began to form in my throat. Clear salty waterfalls fell from my eyes, big ole crocodile tears, enough to fill up a pail. All of those journals were the same in that they told the same story over and over, with the bad outweighing the good. Many of the pages screamed...

HEARTBREAK!

ABANDONMENT!

Broken Relationships!

BEING TAKEN ADVANTAGE OF!

NUMEROUS DEPRESSING AND SELF-CRITICAL THOUGHTS!

Access to the Soul

As I read through the journals, there was laughter mixed with some lament. I was reintroduced to the characters that made up my life story. Even with all the negative stuff I had stored up for many years, with all the trials and tribulations, I took notice of how much I'd grown. The truth is, I didn't leave any room for the good or the blessings. However, I was released from my sleep and became aware. I instantly noticed a detrimental cycle that needed to be broken. I was my worst critic, and this kind of thinking had to end!

The smell of the wood burning in the family room fireplace filled the air. The crackling sound of the fire sparked an idea. Call me crazy if you will. I grabbed a cardboard box and filled it with every journal that I ever kept, walked over to the fireplace, box in hand, and chucked each journal into the fiery abyss.

I sat and watched page by page, and cover by cover become totally consumed in the orange and yellow flames. I kneeled and glared at the sheets of paper smoldering until they transformed into mere ashes. It was my way of letting go. It was my peace.

Jor'Danna

Lovely Lies

The lonely nights, the empty bed, the many nights I waited by the phone. Waiting to be noticed or thought of, by you. Hoping in my heart that you didn't give my goods to another, but knowing the truth all too well.

No one told me that love would hurt this way. I admired you, but I questioned if and when you'd ever loved me? Since your actions...never lined up with the dreams or visions for our future. I believed in you, waiting for something positive to happen... loving you and giving...

my time...

        my money...

                my mind...

                        my body...

My!

My!

My!

How, I waited on a return of anything I could deposit into this dysfunctional union of two broken people. We were a couple who never should have crossed the boundaries of friendship to fall in love.

Now, I sit here trying to piece together my broken heart, looking at your face while you continue to lie about her. You say she's just a friend, yet a connection exists that we don't have. The picture I view stares back at me of you and her in each other's arms for all of Facebook to see. It is proof of the truth and yet you continue to lie and put the blame on others who,

"Don't want to see us together."

Yes, last night I cried, because I realized that I deserve so much more, and this will be my last cry, over you.

Sharon Payne

Free Admission

DESCENDANTS PAIN

Last night I cried cause you're not around, nowhere near.
Missing you this summer when I turned another year.
I should've, would've, could've said,
"I love you."
Last night, I cried for you.
Last night, I cried because she fights,
He fights, we fight, and you fought a good fight.
Our minds wrestle with death tirelessly each night
for life.
Engulfed in feeling a certain type of way,
I realized I was crying every night for the past few days.
Two nights ago I cried for those who did, so we could,
running for their lives through those dark woods.
After watching yet another film about slavery
I bawled!
We need to show a darker people displaying bravery!
I cried because I kept watching their story
over and over again.
I Think!
How about showing the darker skinned people
winning in the end?
My ancestors lost their lives from
many of their decedent's hands.
Winning awards by the Klan!
I've been crying...
There's gotta be a better plan!
A few nights ago, to hold it in, I tried.

Free Admission

Just couldn't keep my tears inside.
A few nights ago, I cried.
Sadly, I'm closing yet another unfulfilled door.
Trying to find the core of my eagerness
to ignore my calling.
It kept me up all night meditating in the dark.
Earlier that day,
I saw the film about Noah's Ark.
Maybe it was the Rock People!
In the Good book, I didn't remember that part.
Part two will be God's sequel.
I pray and stand with God's People.
I throw my hands in the air, feeling once again,
like life isn't fair.
I cried Tuesday night while reading the newspaper.
The name sounded familiar.
My nose and eyes burned because
I wiped them so much,
I immediately thought of you and your family.
Overwhelmed, it's all a darned disgrace to me!
The youthful are innocently being assassinated
in our streets.
News stories, on repeat, make it hard for me to sleep.
I prayed...
for my soul, He'll keep.
I cried last night cause all the crying
from yesterday made my temples pound.
I'm feeling wayward, lost—then found.
Trying to accept HIS way, often times I cry as I pray.

Sure over happier moments I've cried.
Unfortunately,
this week was not one of those moments.
Coming to the realization, I've been crying
while drinking too much wine.
Trying not to fall victim to the disease that runs through my bloodline.
I wept for many reasons.
Truth is—ups and downs flow through every season.
Although I cry, I never stop believing.
No matter how many cries, when I dry my eyes,
I still thank God for allowing me to see another one.

Kenya Renee

ONE GOOD CRY

One night I came close to losing my mind. It was the time I spent the entire night crying, and I couldn't figure out why. I felt stuck in this dark and horrible place that shouldn't exist, but it does. However, I want to light a candle, strike a match, or find a switch in order to bring light into my darkness at midnight. I call it midnight because of the illusion of death.

I turned around and around, making circles in my mind. How can I end this confusion? I began to cry. I didn't have my cell phone with me. Totally, alone in this place. I cried some more. I fell to my knees out of fear and desperation. My tears are now heavier. I began to cry and scream for help, in a tone that got louder and louder. No one answered me.

HELP ME! HELP ME! I SCREAMED AT THE VERY TOP OF MY VOICE, and **STILL NO RESPONSE.**

I got quiet. Just at that moment in my silence, I heard the words.

HeLP Me! HeLP Me! HeLP Me!

I realized it was my own voice. It was an echo. I sunk into despair, not knowing where I was or what to do. I cried louder, as though something would change. There was no where else to go. I immediately found a hidden space within my mind. My place of discovery. I observed my skeletal self. I grabbed hold of a rope. I began to feel light and lifted. My screams and cries grew louder and louder. Finally, I reached the end of my lift.

"I don't know where I am!"

I screamed but without tears or sound. I checked my mouth. It remained wide open. I touched my lips once more and found them still apart. How could that be? I don't know what happened. I felt very sad and hurt. I have to find out why I felt that way. They say there's a place we travel to when distressed, afraid, angry, and outraged that is beyond our understanding, and we often don't know how

we got there. Sometimes it's a protective force, divine intervention, or an encounter that sustains us through it all. Nevertheless, the experience is real, eventful, and can be forever lasting in our lives. Many times the things that we experience are so distinctive and overwhelming that we give them meaning that causes us to lose our grip on reality. Many call this the twilight zone. I believe this was the space I reached when I cried last night. When my tears became nonproductive, and my sound unheard, my pain took me one step beyond.

As time passed, I realized that I was no longer in the same danger, but I continued to hear myself screeching on the inside. I would hear those inner screams, and they took me back to that deep, dark moment when all I knew was to look inside. Ever since then, when those feelings try to reoccur, I receive inspiration from a little nursery rhyme I remember as a child called "Dem Bones." Singing it helps me realize that if we have the urge to cry when there is no apparent threat it's because it's a natural part of life, and it keeps us emotionally healthy. Last night I cried, but I know that my crying was not in vain, and the painful remorse of the past is reaching its final purge. Yes, indeed, the price was paid, and the product is freedom. It is total liberation from carrying a heavy mental and emotional load and comfort for the sorrow connected to it. I perceive that the list of liberties that I have obtained from this discovery is just beginning. As I take a deep cleansing breath, I completely release the fleeting feelings of frustration that once trapped me.

That was one good cry, and my tears sedated my fears. Those tears were an awesome benefit because they left me calm, and I realize that I don't have to deal with this pain. I no longer have to endure the sadness, the tears, the numbness and the revelation is my surrender.

Pamela S.B. Fagen

RECONNECTION TO REALITY

It's a new year, and I must face reality. The actuality of my withdrawal from life was facing me. You wouldn't believe the things that have happened. My oldest daughter, Timerria left home on her 17th birthday. Boo, she told me I mourned too long for you, and she had to experience life away from the nest. You weren't here, my dear best friend, and I had to be strong in my weakness. It is hard to believe that first you left then my baby left, both ribs of my ribs. What a year! Although my friends and family were supportive as I worked through these experiences, my pain of your passing was ever present.

Out of the blue, I also lost my cousin, the comedian of our family. Without any warning, she was gone in the wind. Although it was summer, the wind blew so strongly it continued to make it hard for me to breathe. And to think, I had to move forward with working and existing on auto pilot, while providing care for WinterStarr and the day-care children.

My life took another hit. Granny fell and hard this time, so hard that we had to place her into a nursing home. There was nothing more I alone could do for her. Timerria, her great granddaughter, refused to believe granny was so ill. Her heart was too broken to deal with it, so she stayed away.

Boo, although you're not here, guess who brought her home? Our baby Parisha. I called Timerria to ask if she was okay with Parisha moving in with me, and guess what her response was? Timerria said,

"Ma, I always knew this would happen. I just didn't know when. Will we share a room?"

Boo, did you hear that? She's also coming home. I have always believed that our relationship was a gift from God. I knew ever since the first day, I met you, in high school, as you were about to attack that girl for saying, "Yo mama," I had no clue then what our Creator was doing. I'm just happy

I listened, because never would I have known I would be the god-mother to your daughter. I tell you I can accept anything that comes my way on your behalf! We are sisters, not by our blood but by Jesus' blood! I'm crying as I type this because this is fresh. I hadn't practiced this part, but I trust God. Kizzy, I miss you so much. I love you Boo. You are teaching me even through your death!

Well, Granny died on December 2nd, it was your baby Kassandra's birthday. Was this a sign? I often wonder if your spirits have connected. I cry...wondering if you brought Granny home with you.

My friend, I want you to know that your girls are beautiful! You did an amazing job raising them. Parisha is getting by with the loss of you! She's doing better than you did with the lost of your mom, Boo! She's made mistakes, but you would be proud that she is as strong as you wanted her to be! Kassandra keeps me smiling. She's such a doll! That Nyssa is you all over again. I laugh as I say so, Boo. She's has that same fighting spirit as you had when I met you! I will survive! WinterStarr speaks of you highly. She misses you, and Timerria adores you!

I wish I could have another conversation with you, I wish...I wish I knew what your thoughts were, so I cry. I cry because I don't...

Katerria "Starr" Doty

Free Admission

MAMA

Mama, I love you so much
How I miss you so.
Mama, I called on you, did you hear me?
Did you hear me cry?
I need you, and I want you,
but God knows best.
So, Mama,
make sure you have a talk to our Father.
Please let Him know, they need me here,
and I will make him proud.

Kizzy Givens

MY PEOPLE ◆ MY SINS ◆ MY TRIUMPH

Suddenly,
The tears fall.
Society encourages a man to hold them back at all cost.
How can I?
Since I also embrace my mother's DNA.
I found out what it was like last night.
My people
continue to
disappoint me, while in my sleep.
While in my daydreams, during my attempts not to weep.
In a world
full of parenting dreams,
where the foster care system is the new big money scheme.
Can't lose,
Because she has emotional disorder blues.
Make sure you grab one of them special needs buggeroos.
Didn't do much with your own boys, but this one has aggressive issues.
Cha-ching!
2 new pairs of shoes.
Another 3 teens laid to rest over the weekend.
Gunned down after a late-night party
that momma said they couldn't attend.
You know,
I mean,
they gotta have some kind of life.
Ended too soon, it's not right.

Free Admission

4 preachers and their flock,
flocked to the nearest police station.
Positioned to protest about their lack of presence.
5 days later the nephew of the victim's grandmother is arrested.
The baby's bullet was meant for his pubescent frame.
6 hours... She cries.
For the next 6 minutes... I cry.
Young folks and too much access.
Wish I could bottle it and
call it Flip Juice.
The new and improved pimp's noose.
Instead of the creativity and imagination necessary for survival,
they rely on the next hanging verb that'll get them to a place of rival.
Their noses are in the ass of the sheep in front of them.
I look in the mirror
to make sure I don't mimic my old man's statements verbatim.
And even though I can't replace him,
his rhetoric becomes my anesthetic.
It numbs me
for what I witness younger than 21.
The prescribed meat
on a 19 year old's head is so not Grade A.
In fact, it's riddled with 17 parasites
that feed from a special brand of shit that's made of vapor.
15 paper-thin fools
physically punish 1 dude
because he stood for educational justice
and took his books home from school at night.

Access to the Soul

13 people
abuse their 1st amendment rights
to film it on their flamboyant cellphones
continuing with their highfalutin conversations.
11 overtime hours,
it took for their parents to purchase them…
With debt due.
Only 9 days for these future producers
to reach astronomical internet views.
7 culprits
are suspended from school,
while parents of the other
5 threaten to run for the board
just to oust the administration
if they reprimand their children in any way.
By the way,
3 weeks go by
til the day someone reveals it was all over
1 girl
who said she liked thugs.
I saw her cry after she had her baby.

And I still count the times I've cried.

Todd Parker

> "To accept ourselves as we are means to value our imperfections as much as our perfections."
>
> ~Sandra Bierin

Admit

2

The Body & Soul Speaks

- **Windows Of The Soul**, Sharon Payne *28*
- **Wiser**, Todd Parker *30*
- **My Curves**, Sharon Payne *33*
- **Mouth**, Kizzy Givens *34*
- **Skin**, Kenya Renee *35*
- **Mahogany Crown**, Jor'Danna Davis *36*
- **Bad In A Good Way**, Pamela S.B. Fagen *38*

WINDOWS OF THE SOUL

The body part I would like to embrace is my eyes. When I was growing up, I was always made fun of about my eyes. I was called Pop-Eye, Bug-eyed, and every other eye name, you could think of that meant you had big eyes. I remember being very sensitive about it and would cry about the teasing.

As I grew older, it became clearer, than when I was younger, that big eyes are a popular Payne trait in my family. It is our heritage from my mother's side. There are plenty of people in my family whose eyes are just as big—cousins, siblings, and even my son. With my maturity, came the acceptance of my enlarged opticals. They're the first thing that people notice about me, and they tell me all the time how beautiful they are, and I just smile.

Now I'm getting closer to 50, and I have trouble seeing and reading. I wear bifocals to help while I'm on the computer. My eyes are more precious to me each day. I no longer take them for granted, and I love getting up in the morning looking out the window to see the sun, birds, and nature. I love looking at the rainbow after a thunderstorm or the stars and the moon at night.

I love my eyes. They hold what's in my heart and help me to express how I am feeling. Eyes are the windows to our souls.

Sharon Payne

Valerie Winkfield

WISER

The cruel, harsh reality of kids trying to jockey for a higher position on the ladder of popularity is fierce. So cruel, so harsh, attention is the prize usually gained at the expense of another person's inner security.

"HEAD MO-LODDIE, MO HEAD THAN BODY!"

There went my confidence. Right out the first-grade window. My head didn't look that big to me. Especially since it was the only one that I had. Not much I was able to do about it, except cry every single time. My doubts about going a day without hearing of it were met. Those tears were hidden most of the time because my own family had free rein of inflicting emotional pain. It wasn't their intentions of course, but I blamed my dad for much worse. My older brother had a loaf-o-bread head, and he was the spitting image of him. That fate created more hate for those who chose to spearhead some cracks. Gramps didn't even know he was cutthroat when he told me,

"Boy, you got a grade big ole head!"

Well, I must have one then. I viewed others as having the perfect cranium as long as it didn't resemble mine. And those who had a resemblance of my affliction had other things going for them that thwarted the overload of pot shots I had to endure. They had choices for sure. Maybe it was their athletic prowess, their above average height, or even the laurels of an older sibling. I had to dig deep to withstand the absence of all of those attributes. Sure, I played sports decently enough, but only because I took the periodic advantage of there not being enough players to fill a team. Tough skin became my mainstream. The classroom came with readied ease.

It certainly didn't assist me in fighting off the future comedians who felt it necessary to ridicule my intelligence. I give a thousand thanks to that fateful older, respected athlete who launched a campaign to send me to "Morehead State University." That took a minute to register at the ripe age of 12. But, of course, the pony league baseball team had the most fun with that on-field chatter, rather than your typical, "Hey batter, batter!"

My bloom was beyond late, even similar to a prom date that was coaxed to attend with someone for the poor big headed boy photo.

Barely touching 5 feet in growth, I began high school with an attitude of new beginnings. It involved every single, solitary attempt to hide the extra circumference of my dome. That included very specific haircuts. Although, many said it took an obese man's belt to set the mark for the teenage fade. I wore hats when I could. Button-down shirts with the first three buttons undone. True, it was quite Saturday Night Feverish. But I created the illusion of a not-that-bad-of-a-head extension when I fashioned the collar away from my neck ever so. I reveled in the times in which the swing of growing pains swayed in my favor. They were few and far between, yet, there were some to savor. Surely I shouldn't be able to fit the one size fits all head gear. With new-found confidence, I tried them on. I even had room to spare. While two other guys, the hat didn't treat so fair. Victory. Let the roasting of the little fellow come to an abrupt cease. It did, but only to begin the notion of my alien nation heritage. That bloodline was apparently unconcealed the minute he suggested I was son of "Gazoo." Yes, the green over helmeted sidekick of "Fred Flintstone."

With all the comforting endeavors of the woman who birthed me that I would eventually grow into it, I still dreaded the introductions and profile views that followed. The lack of female appreciation was often masked with semi-believable excuses. Until she came along and flat-out revealed to me why she couldn't be the one to hold my hand. The haircuts, loose shirts, and neck positioning had worn thin. The gene had been passed on to many of my

Free Admission

extended, younger male family members by now, and there was no escaping it. Due to this unwanted legacy, I had to set the tone of acceptance for these young men after me. I had to become an example of strength for them to get through tough days of isolation, even when it is so easy to point out that there are others with over extended brain housing.

Dr. Milo was the anthropology professor by demand. He presented the notion of early scientists that those with perfect skulls were the wisest of the land. "Perfect skulls" meant early humans with a very large brain case. I traveled through the virtual time machine of my formidable years. My skull had to be large enough for my mind that would soon shock, advise, coach lead, entertain, teach, model, acquaint, make peace, and trail blaze.

I can't recall the night before waking up to finally growing into it. But that morning, afternoon, and evening of introductions felt very refreshing.

My profile didn't seem as bad as before, after many conversations. My mind, like a muscle, became my show piece. In the past, it was buried amongst the guys who bore early mustaches, played center in junior high, and were acceptable freaks of nature. I had something that I was proud of, especially since it was mine to keep. Looks fade, muscles plateau, and custom hats are all the rage. Behold, a beautiful skull and a descendant of the well-respected "Caucus Mountains."

Todd Parker

Access to the Soul

MY *Curves*

Over the years, I've learned to embrace my curves. When I was a young girl, I was small, but as a pre-teen in the sixth grade, I started to fill out. Most girls were flat-chested and certainly didn't have hips or thighs, but not me. God saw fit to set me up for a teen life of teasing from friends as well as family. I hated the boys who popped my bra-strap or pat me on the behind as I bent over in my locker to get my books.

When I got to high school, I was a size 12 with a 36 C bust, an ample behind, thighs, and hips, but no stomach. It was just too much to bear. I don't know what was worse—the constant attention from the guys or the jealousy from the girls.

It was also the beginning of molestation by a close family member. I was convinced that how I looked played a major part in it, and I blamed myself for years because I had a woman's body in a girls world. I despised my curves, the attention I got, and the shame. Being unable to walk down the street without getting googled was extremely upsetting. I would go home and cry constantly. Then I started trying to make myself look ugly by overeating or picking at pimples on my face, knowing it would leave scars. I remember thinking I just want to be left alone, but yet I felt so lonely during that period in my life.

Now that I am older, I am more at peace with my life as well as my curves. From the molestation, rape, and ridicule to the life I have now, I'm very proud of myself. I no longer feel the need to hide behind mu mu's. I enjoy buying clothes and looking nice, accentuating every curve. I embrace my big derriere, my thick thighs, and my 46 triple D's. I no longer feel the need to be less than what I am…beautifully blessed, pleasantly plump, and wonderful inside and out. Yes, I embrace my curves—they make me who I am today.

Sharon Payne

Free Admission

MOUTH

Kizzy Givens

SKIN

I love the skin I'm in.
I didn't always feel this way.
In the early 1990's,
I began to love my color in every way.
Maybe because once I entered college,
all men were looking my way.
Even now, every day, so what can I say.
Here's just a little of what I hear
once I pass their way:
Dark n' Lovely
Pretty for a dark skinned girl
Brown Sugar
Sister
Sweetie
Chocolate
Black is Beautiful
Cocoa
Queen
Mocha
Midnight
Shadow
I love your skin
Black Beauty
You're a cutie

I love the skin I am in!

Kenya Renee

MAHOGANY CROWN

I had ill feelings toward my mahogany crown, the crown that adorned my head for my whole existence. After all, it had sharp thorns. Who would want a crown with sharp thorns? I often wondered why I was selected to wear such a crown. After all, it didn't match me. At least that was what I was told. It wasn't anything like the crowns that adorned my mother or my sister's head. Since it looked like I was stuck with this crown, I developed a sense of urgency about making some alterations to it.

It went through a journey of teasing, straightening, braiding, twisting, pressing, cutting, and curling. If I remember correctly, I believe I had my first perm at the age of seven. When I was between 11 and 12 years old, my grandmother made a suggestion that would haunt me for most of my childhood. She was so worried about the thorns in my crown that she suggested my mother take me to a salon and get my crown minimized to a small fro and have the stylist add a Wave Noveau. This may have gotten rid of the thorns but it added to the bag of jokes others carried with them to insult my beauty. I was called everything from "drip drip" to "Jheri Curl girl". Mind you, this was long after the Jheri Curl was in style. We're talking 1995. By the time I was a preteen, with what little confidence I had left, I decided to take control of my crown and I let that Wave Noveau grow out so I could be "normal" again.

The years that would follow were filled with visits to the beauty shop in which I would often hear, "What are we gonna do with this," or "What happened?" I was even told that I needed to visit a doctor because something must be wrong. As the years rolled by, it started to look like all hope had been lost. My crown became fragile, and many of the thorns even fell out! There was nothing I could do to get rid of this stupid crown!

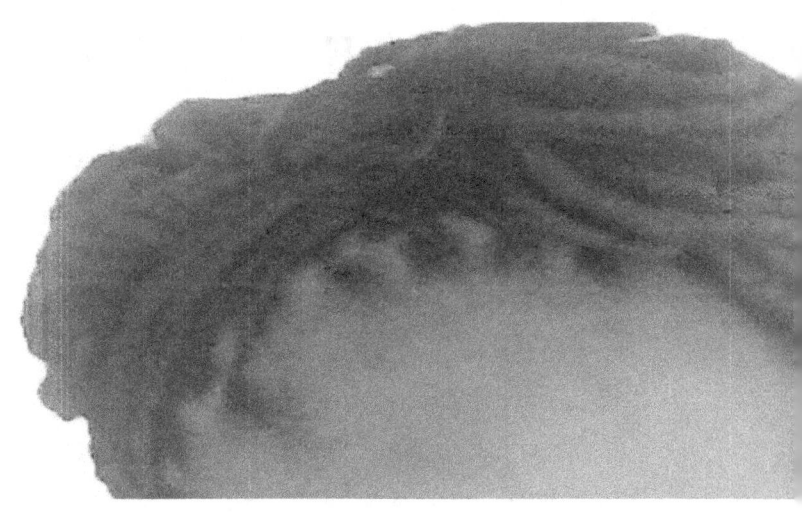

"Something has got to give!"

"Something has got to give!"

I yelled at the woman in the mirror staring back at me. After partaking in deep reflection, I had an epiphany. I realized that my mahogany crown was a blessing in disguise. It was an heirloom passed down to me by my ancestors. It was thicker than most people's crown, and it had an array of beautiful colors such as red, brown, honey blonde, and black. My crown was not made up of sharp thorns, it was made up of tiny ringlets. I asked myself why I hadn't noticed this before. It was time to loc the crown up and leave it be.

Although, it wasn't the easiest decision to make, I knew it was time to end the horrific journey. It was time to embrace the power of my mahogany crown! As I walk around rocking my mahogany crown in its natural form, it is the center of conversations and inspirations.

Jor'Danna

BAD IN A GOOD WAY

On an early evening in the fall of 2014, I received a piece of writing in the mail for critique. I was surprised that it was an exposé about me. The assignment requested that I read and approve an article written by someone who claimed to have knowledge of me. As I read the article, I realized that the writer had distorted the truth a great deal. I sat holding a document that I needed to give advice on, but I had to question the reason for this article. I wondered why they wrote it that way, and I had to make some quick decisions about it.

The article made my character appear to be that of an awful person. It depicted someone who was out to do terrible things and hurt people. By contrast, I've always seen myself as one wanting to do the right thing for myself, my family, and my fellow man. The character that the article portrayed was self-serving and puffed up. Again, many inaccuracies were noted. I've always considered myself as a person who doesn't fabricate or think more highly of myself than I should, I also don't expect more from others than I am willing to give. **I saw myself as a person who strives to do the right thing and who aims to live life to the best of my ability. Don't get me wrong, I am far from perfect, but personal perfection and doing the right thing are very different concepts.**

I gave some reflection to this idea and knowing how I am. I questioned the article's sources. So, I contacted the senders of the document. Those responsible for the article informed me that they were selling a character, and they wanted that character to be me.

"Excuse me," I said.

"Why do you want me to be or portray a negative personality type? Since it's a character so far from who I am, why don't you just call it a work of fiction?" I asked.

Needless to say, the creators of the article and character builders were not happy. In fact, they were pissed.

"Why," I asked?

"You are free to create whatever you want, but it just isn't who I am. It's an interesting character. It's well written, and it's just not me."

Those responsible for the article began to lash out against me for questioning them.

My spirit was momentarily crushed. I had to rush off to that personal place and give myself a value assessment. I thought *It's a new day now.* And it was clear to me that, although I was in the right place, I was definitely wearing the wrong character. Undoubtedly, this experience moved me. It took a tremendous amount of soul searching and remembrance of the power of good before I once again could affirm the realization that one had nothing to do with the other.

In the end, the article didn't get published after all. However, I struggled for some time with this difference of opinion. I pondered whether I took it the wrong way. Maybe I should have gone about it differently since it was simply a role that they wanted me to play. I took it as a personal attack against my character when it was only a persona that they were looking to create. I mean, people believe what they want. The audience is looking for drama, conflict, and a juicy story. Plus, sometimes fitting in is good. Then I came to my senses and knew that I made the right choice because I would have gone along with the deception that they wanted to create, and that's not a character I want to present. That's not an equitable trade-off at all. So, I'm a bad person for not going with the flow. Isn't it ironic that I have to become bad to be good in the eyes of the bad?

Pamela S.B. Fagen

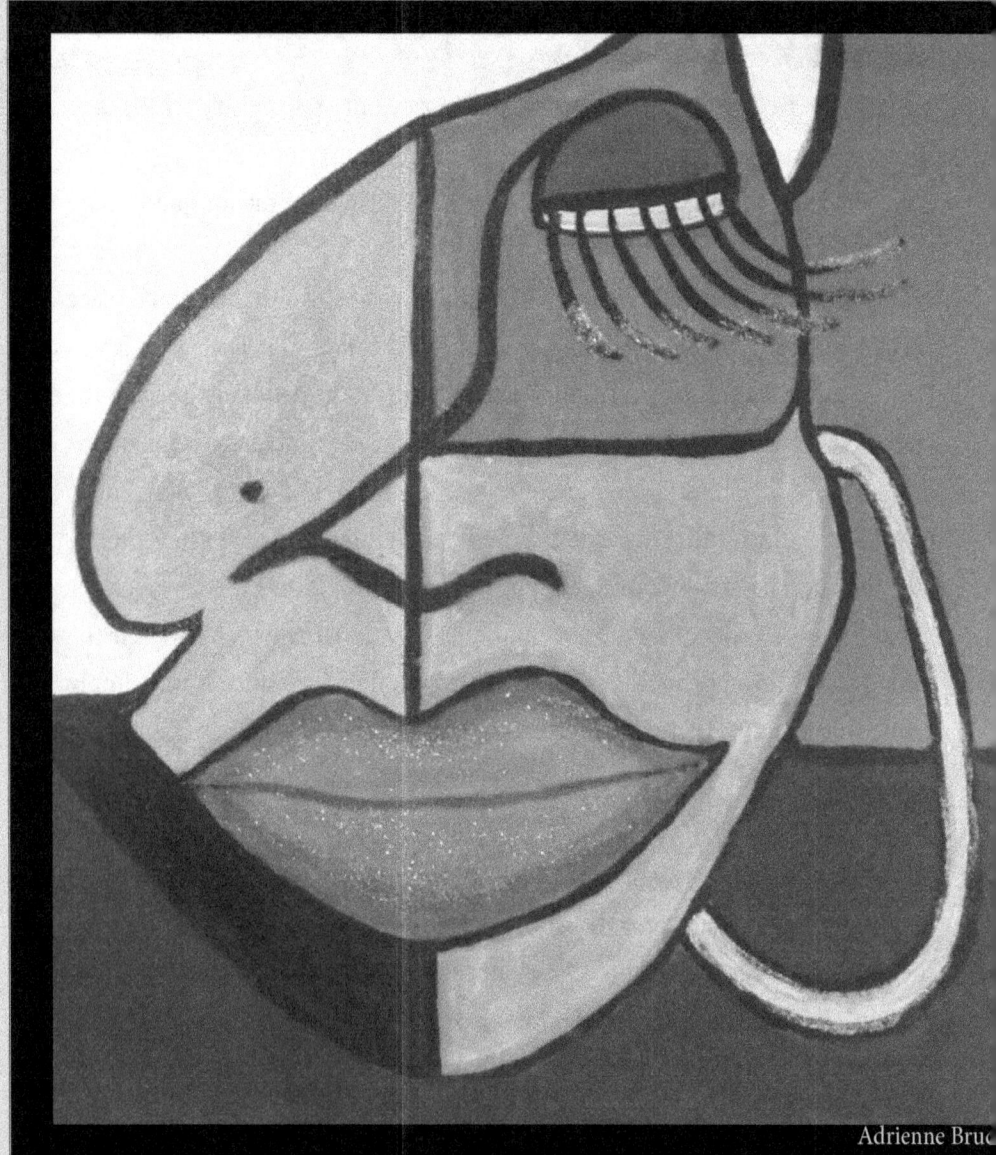

Admit

3

Bitter Sweet

- A Missed Moment, Kenya Renee *42*
- Even For Breakfast, Todd Parker *44*
- Good Morning Sunshine, Kizzy Givens *47*
- Reality At Thirty, Jor'Danna Davis *48*
- WinterStarr, Katerria "Starr" Doty *50*
- A Seasoned Journey, Pamela S. B. Fagen *52*
- Ode To A Fallen Generation, Sharon Payne *56*

A MISSED MOMENT

I will never forget the day,

that moment you came my way.

I traveled over 700 miles just to capture a glimpse to see

if you'd choose me.

Call me a dreamer.

We have so much in common...

starting around the same time,

similar grinds,

both spending our hard-earned and last dimes

to make our dreams viewed in reality times.

I want your story to be mine.

In the process of my quest,

I'm confident because I'm blessed.

I'm artistically dressed,

ready to impress,

daydreams of meeting you at best.

I've worked hard for this; I'm ready for the road test.

Well, three or more months go by,

I finished my produced stage show,

so I'm surely flying high.

No longer do I think of you daily, (Oxymoron)

Access to the Soul

I know I should be ready.

Countless nights I've thanked you in advance,

hundreds waiting for the chance,

and you chose me!

Honestly, when I heard the news,

I was happy I finally paid my stage fright dues.

But my emotions began fighting one another. I'm now feeling the blues.

Desperate, frantic conversations, hoping my quest wasn't in vain,

my happiest moment, so bittersweet, it fills my heart with piercing pain

of missing the opportunity for a featured role on

Tyler Perry's "House of Payne."

A few days too late, a shot at fame cut short,

all because I didn't answer the phone.

Tons of messages unchecked, often,

simply because I hate hearing my ringtone.

Tears fall from my eyes even to this day

because that one opportunity was blown away,

due to that weakness of mine.

But at the same time,

I'm thankful in knowing I'm talented, and that's not mistaken.

I will continue to believe my dream is a reality in the making.

Kenya Renee

EVEN FOR BREAKFAST

Maturity: it takes a lot of this to develop an ego. I have always been proud of it, even now. But not like during our summer vacations. Especially, on this particular trip that we shared with grandad because he didn't have much time left.

We prepared ourselves for the Memphis trek. It was time, right? He's in a wheelchair now, so it's not like we can play catch like we used to, since his sight is a thing of the past. However, passing on is worse. Sometimes, I wish he could be active enough to have fun, but besides that, I'm in the 8th grade. I'm grown!

As I crept up to his awaiting, smirkish grin, he excited me with,

"I got yo Pepper."

I was seven years old all over again. Couldn't wait to crack open an ice cold one. Even for the most important meal of all, I couldn't wait. (Breakfast). Rarely did he let me see the bottom of that case. I could have as many as I could handle. He kept them in a small corner-store cooler that stayed on the back of his pickup. You know, the driveway play lot. Same place where it was routine to sit and slice the peaches from the tree in the backyard and next door (but only if the neighbors weren't home). Even though, I didn't think they'd mind.

I stashed my case of June's good memories on the side of the concrete porch. This custom was as normal as tank tops and two dollar sandals. Are you wondering why I am getting so excited? Well, other soft drinks were enjoyable, but this was caramel-flavored music to my ears. I invited that cold drink to give my body a shock. I can even claim the consumption with a pack of Pop Rocks. (Just one time though).

My mom, his daughter, called me into the house from off the platform stoop. I guess she was testing me to see if I knew. Just for her spirit to sit well, she wanted me to talk to grandad for a good spell. As the soda tickled my taste buds we talked about old times, his and mine. Remember, I'm grown too. **I cherished his southern-sounding "Ya know whats." They managed to travel slowly through his sunken face and drooping jowls. From his, "Boy, you got a grade big ole head!"**

I would only accept that from him. Frankly, it was because he had one too.

His head displayed a clean collegiate cut with a shadow of trepidation. He could barely keep it leveled during any lengthy conversation. I went to get another 12 ounce as he struggled to the bathroom. I wound up assisting him. His right side wasn't as strong as it was in years past, but he insisted on trying to one-arm it.

I noticed the rott-gutt in his lap, which usually meant a nap was coming. Had to help him twist the cap.

"Po a lil' bit of that Pepper in there boy."

Like any youngster at the time, I did what I was asked. Despite the dread of leaving my friends behind, it was peaceful for me to perform the tasks.

Anything for him, but I so freely took those moments for granted. Life's many doses of irony. Right then, I knew there would be no repeat of this routine next summer. This trip was special, a call for me to write it down later. Reminiscing in the present, the sun-filled sky, crickets in harmony, good fishin', and water bug kitchen scatter. It didn't matter. I had the cold satisfaction of a Pepper, for breakfast.

I didn't realize then how strongly attached the flavor of the liquid was to my inner soul. At times, I wonder if grandad knew what he was doing. Probably a little bit. I know grandparents have their "spoil-my-grandkids" duties. But was he laying the foundation of lasting memories? Surely.

I live in his generosity and calm. He was a man of distinction. I wish he hadn't left so soon. The selfish man-child within me would have loved to reach his pinnacle of expressing how heavy that taste of Dr. Pepper soda was for me. But

Free Admission

he translated that to me, and without words, just a nod. Even for breakfast.

That was a long drive back home to Chicago. There was plenty of room in the minivan for my surplus supply of sugary joy. I checked back there often. More often than I ever did anything else. Anything. Didn't think holding snapshots of someone in my mind was existential. Grandad's greeting, his battle with laughter, his colorful banter, the people that respected him. Those that neglected him. A full life he had lived. I should maximize more genes since I know what they are responsible for.

More quality friendships…
Grateful mornings…
Genuine greetings and meaningful farewells.

For starters, I'll keep **Dr. Pepper** in business whenever I have a chance. I'll enjoy the swirling red of the logo before the tingling cold from its temperature treats my hand.

It's like those memories were meant to leave a bitter feeling, unlike the taste. That maintains the snapshots of a man that I must continue to celebrate—a grandfather's job well done.

"Yeah, you can have one, man."

Even for breakfast.

Todd Parker

GOOD MORNING SUNSHINE

Thank you my Lord for blessing me

with another day of Your glory,

Your strength, and also, my mind, Lord.

I'm so grateful to have been out last night to see "The Wiz"

and a week ago India Arie.

I couldn't see anything but a glare or shadows…funny.

I had to depend on my ears to see.

But the God I serve brought me through the pain

and showed me just who is in control once again.

I heard the wonderful messages that were told,

the voices singing through song were bold.

I imagined all the faces expressed emotionally.

To me these experiences were extremely enlightening.

I thank you again for a wonderful day and a night on the town.

Keep the blessings coming 'cause I will not let you down.

Love Kizzy ♥

REALITY AT THIRTY

The year was 1983,

and then there was me.

Eyes closed yet to be introduced to the world.

No mistakes, no regrets, no hurts, and no shame

Happy in my birthday suit,

hadn't even been given a name.

Thirty years later, eyes wide open.

I ask myself, "Have I arrived?

Even though, I'm still not satisfied?!"

My thirtieth is fast approaching

and although I'm disappointed,

God, how happy I am to be alive.

Another day, another chance.

My own voice drowns out my thoughts,

"Count your blessings!"

The problem is that I can't help but to think about my circumstances.

In reality at thirty,

shouldn't I be over my hurts and pain?

Had all my living been in vain?

To all of those on the outside looking in,

Two days before reality at thirty,

some fool took all my stuff.

The stuff I worked so damn hard for.

Broke in and entered my life

right through my front door!

Seven months into reality at thirty,

I had no place to call my own,

a few dollars to my name.

Feeling extremely stressed but not alone.

It's hard, because there's no one to blame.

When I started to question what the hell is going on,

my mother's voice creeps in.

"It could be worse child,

lift up your head and smile."

I fall to my knees and ask God, "Help me please."

I'm not settling for this reality at thirty!

Jor'Danna

WINTERSTARR

My most bitter-sweet moment was... taking a pregnancy test after "*Grey's Anatomy*" ended to find Jackie say, "I'm not playing, you're pregnant!" The thought of being pregnant was both elating yet appalling! The truth is I wanted another child. I never wanted to have one child in this world without a sibling. As much as I wanted another child, never did I want to procreate another child with my first love, my ex-husband! There I said it, "ex-husband." How did I get back to this place? How did I drop the ball? Why did those sperm cells connect to my eggs but the sperm cells from others never attached themselves? To be truthful, I believed I couldn't conceive another child, for I'd had some pretty sure oops over the years, to no avail.

After the initial shock wore off, and I realized there is a baby forming in this belly of mine: flipped emotions...happy then sad. Happy because I can conceive; my first born will not be alone in this world after I'm gone. I also now have a chance to better my parenting and effectively guide this new child, knowing more than I did; making better choices than I had, and applying my wisdom to this person's life. I was able to embrace my pregnant belly with my daughter Timerria by taking some of the most beautiful pregnant pictures I've ever seen. I even learned to be accepting of this unborn child. I began preparing for the grand entrance of little WinterStarr's life.

My delivery was planned. I told myself not to focus on the pain, yet focus on the dedication of WinterStarr to God. I had no drugs to take the pain away. I took breaths through each contraction.

I blessed and prayed over every medical attendant and family member present to create a safe, loving environment, and I presented WinterStarr back to God who created her.

I've heard that **before babies are born they choose their parents.** So I'm up for that assignment! Now that I embraced the emotions I shared with you, I had to also, get over the bitterness of lying down with Tim, unprotected. After all we've been through, all the trials I triumphed! Back to the middle. I say "middle" because the beginning was love. The middle was where I knew that he wasn't for me, and it was just a matter of time.

Now whoever my husband may be. I've brought the unplanned pregnancy, along with this dad, whom I've now reenlisted another 18 years with. I was celebrating because I was almost free from having to be present with him for the sake of our first daughter. I even moved into this house to give our children a chance at a family with mom and dad. Well, for the sake of time, I'll say back to the middle with raising another child.

—fighting for financial assistance.
—fighting to forgive myself for being insane.

Now this is where I am. I still have to remind myself, that I forgive myself. It helps when Starr says mom, "I love you" or asks, "Did I tell you I love you today?"

Katerria "Starr" Doty

A SEASONED JOURNEY

I shut my eyes tightly and began to breathe deeply. I felt like I was resurrected out of my body and came back. I'm excited about taking a flight of an extraordinary journey. The starting point is not yet clear, and the destination is less apparent. Nevertheless, I am about to getaway. I have checked my luggage at the check-in station, and I have a small carry-on. I heard an announcement that it was time to take off.

"Good morning ladies and gentlemen. This is your captain speaking. Thank you very much for joining us today. We will be flying through the Spices of Life. The length of the flight is up to you. We may experience some turbulence as you let go of your old, insignificant memories.

Please keep your seat belts fastened and stay in your seats. Keep the seat trays locked in an upright position as we depart. We'll do everything we can to make your trip an enjoyable one."

I am elated but a little uneasy about the flight. I decide to settle down and give my mind permission to go within, relax, and enjoy the emotional ambiance. The bitter and the sweet.

Feeling relaxed in the comfortable seat, I was startled when the attendant came around and asked if I wanted a beverage. I said, "Yes. I'd like a bottle of water and a bottle of wine."

My mind felt at peace, and I had an appreciation for the kindness of the attendant. I felt alleviated of any anxiety at the moment. I began to slowly sip on the wine and felt relaxed. I started to slip into a state of reflection concerning my life.

I am 60 plus years of age and filled with a multitude of memories, both good and bad. The pleasure of some past experiences and the pain of missing them in my life is what I call bittersweet.

The flight attendant served the four main entrees of life that included the sweet, the bitter, the spicy, and the salty. Some of the four tastes are undesirable and symbolize life experiences. I am in constant search for spices to describe my emotions. However, I've learned that life is about balance. A little spice and sweet can modify bitter or bland tastes. Pursuing a mixture of these flavors and having the balance of them working in harmony is what makes life delicious.

A famous quote enters my mind. "It's better to have loved and lost than never to have loved at all." It is a representation of spicy experiences. I know that they are missing in my life right now. Without these experiences, it is easy to float through life, desiring love and someone to share it with you, constantly seeking love and wanting a demonstration that surpasses all other experiences. It's easy to see the sweetness of love in the lives of others while feeling the bitter sting of love's absence in my own.

During this journey of bittersweet, I came to the knowledge of a grain of truth in the world around me. I am not talking about a 2,000 year ago world truth or a world yet to come, but God's truth that shows itself in my world and my life. Right now, I am solving my own riddles through poetry and short stories.

The sun shined through the window as I reflected and it created pleasant warmth on my face. I continued to speculate on this life that I've lived for 60 plus years. A bittersweet truth revealed itself to me.

"It's all how you see it."

It is not always what appears on the surface or what you feel at the moment. It's not about how a thing looks at the time of its happening that defines it. But many times, the thing you are supposed to see is covered with the thing that's appearing in your life!

I decided to close the window blinds. I cleared my palate with water and began to sip a little more wine as I continued my reflections. I have lived some, and I have a lot of life left. Some things continue throughout life, and some are seasonal. Just when you think you know caring, compassion, humility, and the goodness of mankind, including the many who have died before us. Just when you feel you understand the expectations of freedom, that is when life throws a curve.

Just at that moment the flashing lights went off, and the attendant said, "Please finish your beverages and make one last trip to the lavatory." I began to drink the last of my wine and thought about the game of life and how it is to be played. I began to reflect on the salty focuses of the present. We compete over aptitude, beauty, power, money, and the list goes on. We judge each other by the standards we've set. Whatever situation we are in, we want to have the better end of bondage or liberty. There is extreme bitter and sweet with each one.

We endure the bitterness of persecution that is designed to tear us apart, like a torn cardboard box. We are courageous even though the sour and salty mix of vinegars in life invades our world, seeking to change, compromise, and reduce us to nothing. Who declares that I am placed on the bottom of the food chain? When we see it for what it is, we no longer ask the question, "Why me?" But, instead we seek God for greatness. We gain strength. We ask God to reveal to us this importance, which requires us to suffer such persecution, the type of persecution befitting only those in extreme power.

I know the sweet taste of victory. I begin to ask God to show me how to turn the salty tears of persecution into power. I've got my own personal cheer going on inside, with these sweet words "RAH! RAH! RAH!" Unfortunately, just when I'm filled to the brim with overcoming power and excitement, it happens—the wind of bitterness blows.

The combination of the bitter taste of a fearful moment reveals that my persecutors want to wear my desires, my hopes, my dreams, and my fight. They want to be me. This is the idea of fear spoken of in ancient times. There is nothing new under the sun. I ask a question, "Is this FALSE EVIDENCE

APPEARING REAL?" In an act of surrender, I stretch my arms outward and upward as I ask God, "IS MY LIVING IN VAIN?" And is yours. The answer that I received is enlightening.

"Never are you to forget that the sun shines on the just and the unjust."
Consider this riddle: I never was, and always will be. No one ever saw me, nor ever will, and yet I am, the confidence of all, to live and breathe on this terrestrial ball. I'm not E. T. What am I? (TOMORROW)*

The attendant came through one more time and said, "I will take your garbage now. Raise your seats and tables to an upright position and secure your seat belts. We will be landing soon."

I took the last swallow of water and gave her the empty bottle. I realized that this was a good flight. I gave myself free admission to reflect upon what it means to have bittersweet memories. I concluded my reflections by realizing, I don't have just one bittersweet moment. This present life is but a moment in time. Time itself is a riddle and is not to be mistaken for the doctrine of seasons. Plotting your course in life is no different than embarking on a long flight.

Here's where the flight metaphor really breaks down. Unlike a flight, our journey in life has no ultimate end point. There are always new skills to develop, new subjects to learn, and new opportunities to explore. I guess that knowledge is both the bitter and sweet. Now, how much you enjoy the journey and how far you will travel is up to you.

"We are now landing. Thank you for flying with us. We hope you enjoyed the flight."

Pamela S. B. Fagen

*www.answerbag.com/q_view/437076

ODE TO A FALLEN GENERATION

My view of the world has sadly changed.

The destruction of youth is insane.

There is

No Respect!

No Character!

No Pride!

And those underwear!

I wish they would hide!

In my day, we sang the national anthem

with our right arm raised.

We were proud of our country

and in God, we praised.

It all went down the drain when they took prayer out of schools,

made spankings against the rules,

and left kids home,

alone to roam.

They took fathers to jail

Moms' working day and night as well.

To put food on the table

And pay the bills too.

We used to have grandparents

Who invested their time.

Taught us manners and respect

and how to mind.

They let it be known it just wasn't about you,

but you had to be accountable

for everything, you do.

Oh, how my heart breaks cause,

No longer are schools safe.

A bullet you could catch.

They're filled with chaos and anger

and bullies to match.

Where is the village that raised us fine?

Scared to get involved

cause they may do some J time.

Sharon Payne

Admit

4

Forgiving

- On The Battlefield, Pamela S.B. Fagen *60*
- Unconditional Forgiveness, Jor'Danna Davis *64*
- Chin In Your Chest, Todd Parker *66*
- Real Friends, Kenya Renee *69*
- Solved In Love, Kizzy Givens *70*
- The Dad I Never Had, Sharon Payne *74*

Free Admission

ON THE BATTLEFIELD

Come one! Come all!

Faithful troops,

this is an urgent call!

I have something to make clear!

This announcement everybody must hear!

Join with me to arrest the enemies who have stolen much!

Who leaves us lame, maimed and dependent on a crutch!

To this degradation we can undividedly attest!

These painful things I've internalized,

I have to get off my chest.

You falsely accused me!

Your demeanor was extremely negative!

You belittled my character!

You wounded me deeply

Instinctively, the injured returns a hurt for a hurt.

Ironically, you preached an eye for an eye.

But what if the eye you seek is not the eye that damaged you?

You are seeking annihilation and full consumption, it's true.

Thus, I lay wounded on the battlefield attacked.

Lying there to die too wounded to shout!

It appears that the enemy has a need for me not to turn the other cheek and doubt. Except I have not sinned,

Yet, I am the one you mistreat!

You deliberately target me!

You seek to oppress!

You aim to persecute!

Access to the Soul

You want to isolate!

You desire to desecrate!

You have wagered many wars and strategic attacks.

The terrorist is an accuser that seeks to herald the victim's shame.

Counterattack is its focus to inflict more pain.

You are a tenacious enemy that always comes back.

I bleed out on the battlefield.

Have the opponents a need?

They demand denial of the craftiness of evil,

and the haters that perpetuate ultimate greed.

I have not sinned, yet the enemy manipulates.

In an effort to overcome; I refuse this bitter stake.

Evil has turned and accused me again, but this is not my case.

And I was pulled out of its flame...

I refuse to accept defeat!
I am not weak!

This is a race I must run!

My weapon is the Word of the Spirit that I never shun.

I won't relinquish my power!

The drive in me is greater!

I will not wear the menace's label!

I stand to strike the stronghold.

I will not accept being wrongly accused anymore!

Still the enemy is a disrespectful bully who uses my fellow man to carry out its brutality.

You can neither deal with God's presence,

Nor the person He has made me.

A black, educated, and professional, woman,

transformed by the renewing of her mind.

Struggling with salvation but is willing to learn.

She makes a contribution to the world, and her strength is kindness.

The accuser tries to violate me by setting me up to appear lazy,

with believing that unchanged circumstances will drive me crazy.

Being strong, I survived its undeserved hostility.

Despite overcoming their threats these enemies' charge full enmity:

of confusion, despair, uncertainty, and being out of touch with reality.

these are the chosen ingredients of

a simple recipe for mortality.

Thus letting me know, I am still a lit torch on the battlefield of life.

God came to heal me with his stripes...

the adversaries have a need for me not to exist.

But it is NOT they that solidify my sustenance.

The rivals are now on the defensive.

Justifying their destructive incentives,

the likelihood of eradication of every generation is the plot.

Yes, I was wronged,
but **I sinned not.**

The evil force is now saying that the deals of the past,

validate the compensations of present blasts.

Uninvited they invade on our GROUNDS to PLAY.

Falsely, the antagonists claim it's the innocent's price to pay.

Now the wicked want me to cover the cost,

requiring my bondage for yesterday's loss.

Why should I wear the yoke of a lie?

It's not my reality to be beaten and

Access to the Soul

whipped, but never cry?

Mind wondering much until it sees.

It appears that **you owe me!**

How can I forgive when it's hard to live?

I remain on the battlefield of life

and I fight.

With God's help, I can maintain my defense.

Nothing have I done to make this enemy seek recompense.

There is no motive.

My only job is to forgive even if

it doesn't make sense!

I know that God will execute my vengeance!

TO BE CONTINUED...

Pamela S.B. Fagen

JamieLynn Warber

Free Admission

UNCONDITIONAL FORGIVENESS

Protector, provider, you never were.

In and out of my life like a revolving door.

When everyone said,

you didn't deserve the least bit of attention,

a chance was given.

Flashbacks of drunken, high nights,

me hiding in the corner, dodging your anger.

Listening to words that could penetrate

the hardest of hearts.

You let that poison be your inspiration,

the streets your destination.

All I ever wanted was for you

to be at home,

To be my protection from the world,

to hold **me at times when I was alone.**

Out of sight

Out of mind

is how I had to cope.

You missed almost every pivotal point in my life.

Anger is what used to fill the hole in my soul,

but now it's filled with hope.

And hell, that definitely took some growth

I'm often asked...

"Would I give you another shot?"

"Would I do what you could not?"

Understand, being bitter is not what I'm about

Because of you I'm stronger, more resilient, I am me.

My love has no boundaries.

Constant wishes for your success,

although our relationship is not at its best.

Our connection has potential

because my forgiveness is unconditional.

Even though, I cannot forget,

our relationship wasn't traditional

I pray for all wounds to heal.

You are my earthly father that God has chosen.

It is with this strength that I will forgive.

Regretful, some chapters in my life closed,

No blame,

No guilt,

No seeking an apology.

For it is with ourselves that we must live to accept the Saviors theology.

Jor'Danna

CHIN IN YOUR CHEST

A life isn't worth the short breaths
if it doesn't produce the air for others to breathe.
No matter what we undertake as humans,
as humans is how we reprieve.
Elect someone to affect someone.
Nomination domination.
For bay-bee boi.
But this boy has men amongst him that revere him as Pop.
And the women...oh, the women love JP.
They love the man,
They love the carpenter.
They love the financial planner,
The adviser. The teacher. The cat—man.
And don't dare behave in a manner that is uncouth.
Learn how to act. Get your education.
Education for a president.
He even looks like Obama.
He takes good care of his mama.
It's all about love with my mama.
A slight tap upon the bottoms of her pajamas.
For dessert, you get to giggle from his
public announcement of "baby."
Just one real nick off the old block,
but the roots of his campaign extend.
In and beyond NIU, WIU, CSU,
and between me and you,

the reason why earth has 10 better men.
He couldn't and wouldn't allow me to boast my manhood.
Not in his house, on his porch, or in his neighborhood.
He's given me the knowledge but wouldn't let me experience it.
I tried to show him I understand it even though he's old-fashioned.
Too busy trying to be slick after being given it.
I needed to peacock my wisdom,
unlike everyone else in the fam.
Just let me do this life of mine.
No lambs here. I'm a full-grown ram.
It took that same emotional pain
to put together the pieces of building a competitive man.
Couldn't reveal the entire plan.
He refused to reveal the entire plan.
Not until I saw it unfurl from your reservoir as a grand.
Or more like Hell-of-a-father.
I bother him, with good reason, to finally pay attention.
If it weren't about the pen, the paper, the books, then I needn't mention.
He was even the executioner of teenage dreams and inner-city themes.
C'mon Pop. It's not like you listened or explained your decisions.
I could use more than that to navigate these streets.
As your son, the pressures of living up to your glory,
how about I blow it for GP.
I would've done so, you know.
If I didn't realize first hand that this man was in high demand
despite his flim-flam background,
unsound upbringing, and feelings of despair.
He did it with a cucumber cool. And my issue was, no Nikes by the pair.
All this prompted me to say that there's no way

Free Admission

I'm letting myself grow up to be like you.
But who would've knew?
I like jazz.
I love saving money.
I like workin' hard.
I loved graduating with him.
I loved him graduating with me.
New-fashioned, old-school reign.
Got him flowing all thru these veins.
But one fact still remains.
He ain't Mr. Brady.
Little-league game after game and it's a shame he only came to three.
My mirror reflection displays his pride.
I recognize his confidence in my own stride.
I climbed Mt. Forgiveness because it was for our best.
In order for my G.O.A.T to manifest.
I like the man. I love my Pop.
I love the lost memory of calling him anything other than Pop.
I loved the late night haircuts.
I hated the party pick-ups.
I like the father. He is not my daddy.
He is my best friend's guest at his wedding.
He is my Pop. And I love him.

Dedicated for your 60th

Todd Parker

REAL FRIENDS

How many of us have them?

I thank you,

my friends, for all you do,

no matter what!

You are my only crew.

The strength you give me is critical,

and your timing is incredible.

That's why the love and prayers,

I give back to you—my friends are inevitable.

When I exhaled,

you gave me what I needed to prevail

over hurt feelings,

I thank you,

my friends,

for providing me with a bond-filled healing.

You complete my world,

protecting me with your watchful eyes,

Free Admission

often seeing through the bull crap

and so many surrounding scornful lies.

I haven't seen my friends in a really long time.

I think about the days we spent together

and all the good times.

I thank you, friends of my past,

for being there at every nightly show.

Though you were tired,

you never told me no.

When my outlook was down

and I was unable to cope,

my friends from the past certainly were my hope.

You stayed with me through his disappearing acts,

biased in favor of my thoughts.

Those were the necessary facts.

When my vision is clouded by negativity,

it's your eyes I use to detect positivity.

I want to thank you for being there for me

through thick and thin.

I appreciate you for being friends.

As one, we go through many phases,

consoling each other through all the stages.

Many times, up all night, ensuring we are alright.

Our opinions are of a priceless token,

even if the truth is spoken.

As I sit underneath this planted friendship tree,

I carve a saying for each of you

to show just how much you mean to me.

As the streams of life cover me with shade,

I think of your advice 'til this day,

corrected some mistakes I've made.

To all the past and present ones.

Thank you for being my friends.

You are forever in my thoughts until the end.

Kenya Renee

SOLVED IN LOVE

Let's not fight and argue
Let's not do that today.
Let's learn to share our problems
Let's love them all away.

We do not have to quarrel
We sometimes disagree;
We listen to each other
We do this with patience and courtesy.

When we take the time to listen
When we both have had our way.
When can we learn to share our problems?
When can we love them all away?

Life is really much too short
Life groans for us to love and not argue much
Life whispers alternative ways of living in peace
Life demands us to work at our friendships, and let hate cease.

We must not use our time to fuss
We must care or our happiness fades;
We must always share our problems
We must love them all away.

Kizzy Givens

THE DAD I NEVER HAD

> "Dad just passed away this morning! Please come to the nursing home as soon as possible. Call me!"

As I sat there numb reviewing the text in my mind from my brother, I couldn't believe what I was reading. The date was June 10, 2013. How could he die now?

I looked around the conference room, surrounded by my co-workers who had no idea of what just happened. I slowly rose up out of my chair and left the meeting. My heart was heavy, and my thoughts were erratic. Had he suffered or did he go peacefully? I wondered whether he was alone or a nurse was with him. I had to get to a phone. I hurried to my desk to make a call.

"Hello?"

Once again, my brother relayed the message to me that indeed Dad had died. Both of my twin brothers were waiting for me at the nursing home. I told my boss what was going on and raced to my truck. It's funny; I don't really remember the ride. It was all a blur to me. Slowly, I pulled into the parking lot.

The receptionist, Carolyn, looked up from her desk and said, "I'm so sorry about your father!"

"Thank you!" I said. I walked into the lobby, and the smell of disinfectant and old people met me head-on. I walked somberly to the elevator and pressed the number two button for the second floor. As I entered his room, #213, I tried to prepare myself for what I was about to see. My brothers were sitting there waiting for the doctor to sign the death certificate. We hugged. I walked over to his body, which was lifeless and cold. His hands folded on his chest. As I gazed upon him, I thought about how close we had become in his later years. You see, I didn't always love my stepdad. In fact, I can honestly say that I hated him growing up. I looked at him again as we sat in silence. He looked nothing like the man I knew as a child. Sickness had transformed his 6'-7", 200 lb., muscular body into scrawny bones.

I spent a lifetime hating my dad for the things he had done to his family. I detested his violent outbursts, the domestic violence toward my mother, and the physical beatings of my brothers. I suffered the most from the molestation. It played such a major part of who I became as an adult. I suffered hell because of this man and always said that when he died I would spit on his grave. But, none of those feelings came now.

I went through years of therapy and spiritual counseling trying to figure out the "why me's." I struggled to forgive him so I could move on with my life. I was finally at peace and would no longer cry remembering the past. I had come to the conclusion that we are all imperfect somehow. I looked at him again.

I thought back to how he came here. He'd lived alone and had diabetes. He didn't always take his medicine, due to stubbornness. Once when he got up to use the washroom, he fell and broke his neck. He could not move. We'd called him for three days. I remember dad telling us later that he could hear us, but he couldn't reach the phone. Finally, my brother went to his house to check on him because he hadn't called any of us back. Dad was found on the floor in the hallway of his bedroom. He had stayed in the hospital for quite a while because they botched the surgery. He was never able to look down again.

We had to put him in a nursing home, and he hated staying there. We felt so guilty but had no choice since we all worked. Our hopes of him gaining a full, speedy recovery quickly diminished when his health became worse. We learned that he not only suffered from diabetes but also Parkinson's disease and bipolar disorder. Additionally, he had other issues that stemmed from being sprayed with Agent Orange in the Vietnam War. That explained some of the violent outbursts in his younger years.

I remember walking into his room in the nursing home for the first time. He looked at me, and his eyes teared up. I had never seen my dad cry except at his mom's funeral. "Dad, why are you crying?" He gave me a grave look and said, "I didn't think you would come!" I stared at him and said, "Dad, I forgive you!" I held his hand as he turned his head and looked out the window, continuing to cry. We stayed like that for a long time in silence with my hand in his. It was a very emotional moment. I realized it was his way of saying "I'm sorry." I was relieved. All those years, I wondered if he thought it was wrong or felt guilty about it. Did he understand the chaos that he created? Each teardrop that he shed assured me that his apology was sincere, and I knew it was complete.

In the three years of declining health, my dad and I grew close. He shared with me stories of his childhood. He told me about his regrets and his proudest moments. He told me how proud he was of me and how I was a great single parent. He shared with me how much he loved his grandchildren and how proud he was of them going to college and being respectable and smart. We talked about my hopes and dreams for the future. I shared with him my relationship issues with a special someone and money management. We joked, laughed, and talked about old times. We even conversed about God and the Bible. The dad I had always wanted was becoming a reality. I looked forward to our talks when visiting him. He even prayed with me when I faced a promotion and the tough test it took to make it.

Dad's condition grew worse over time. He was always being transferred to the hospital back and forth. One minute it was pneumonia, the next a urinary tract infection or bed sores. It was always something. After a while, his voice became shallow, and you couldn't always understand him. He could no longer walk to the washroom. He couldn't move much, and his hands would shake uncontrollably because of the Parkinson's. He would just motion for us to do things. I began to see the weariness and frustration on his face. It was hard to watch a loved one suffer. My brothers and I took turns so that we wouldn't get worn out. Even though we put those devices in place, we still began to slack off on our visits to the nursing home. The decline of the visits happened close to the end because all he did at that point was sleep. Sometimes I was so tired from the new job that all I could do was sit in the recliner next to him and go to sleep too. I guess I just wanted him to know that someone was there with him in his room.

The nervousness in my stomach signaled that his time on earth was coming to an end. I didn't know the exact date, but I knew it would be soon. God had prepared me for the death. And then the call. It was bittersweet. My dad didn't have to suffer anymore.

I'm so happy that God restored our relationship before he took my dad. I'm grateful to God that I didn't let pride or un-forgiveness stand in my way of getting to know my dad. In the end, God blessed me with the best dad ever.

Sharon Payne

Admit 5

Living Letters

- Bankrupt, Kizzy Givens *80*
- Powerful Black Women, Kenya Renee *81*
- Legacy To My Son, Kenya Renee *83*
- An Elder's Voice, Sharon Payne *82*
- Teenage Me, Jor'Danna Davis *87*
- To Years Past, Pamela S.B. Fagen *90*
- Advice For The Youth, Kenya Renee *94*
- Bro Bigger, Todd Parker *96*
- Dear Daughter, Kenya Renee *98*

Free Admission

BANKRUPT

Well, what did my father do?

He treated me with no respect.

He was so mean to me.

My father treated

people on the street

better than he treated me.

I was "the baby,"

and always wanted

to make him proud,

even though I knew

he did not care,

not one cent!

Kizzy Givens

Photography by EnJay

Access to the Soul

POWERFUL BLACK WOMEN

My provider, no one else's heart is wider than yours;
your house has an open door policy, because you care.
My mother!
You're always there or should I say you are always near to hear.
Silently showing your view—not saying a word when I complain to you.
You know my pain.
When my heart is broken, we have a mutual respect,
even when dialect is not spoken, you are my souvenir.
Possessing no fear is just one of the values you've instilled in me.
Black, you are proud to be.
When I look at you a reflection of greatness, I see.
The bond we have, can never be severed.
Our bond lasts forever.

I can never forget the woman who nurtured me.
It's just a few of us in our family tree.
You mean the world to me.
You continue to guide me through.
I'm writing this poem especially for you.
I love you then, now and always.
I'm proud to be your daughter until the end of my days.
Your footstep traces are hard to follow.
I thank God for you—my role model.
So much, you've sacrificed.
Powerful black woman for life.
Thank you Grandma for showing me how to hustle hard.
Hard you are. You are the family's shining star.
Wearing multiple hats,
holding us down for years and no one can dispute that.

Free Admission

Art by: JamieLynn Warber

Great with your hands;
From quilting, sewing,
cooking, gardening,
just to name a few, and I thank you for leaving a legacy of
stability for our small family line to follow.
Seventy plus seven and some.
Longevity that shows the blessings in your life. Grandma,
I'll be praying for you, like I always do—on my knees tonight!
Powerful black woman for life.
You taught me to love my race.
Such a pretty face once—upon a time.
Aunts, I think of you both all the time.
One here and the other I only see in my dreams.
I cherish how I was raised by you,
my mother and grandmother as a team.
Powerful black women for life.
Some say that
there are some who stick closer to you than family.
You, my godmother and grandmother mean the world to me.
And last but not least, my cousins.
Where would I be without you?
Powerful black women for life.

Kenya Renee

LEGACY TO MY SON

Dear Son,

Let me start by saying, I love you. Listen to the words that are coming out of my mouth. I know what I'm talking about when I say this!

You are magnificent!
You are debonair!
You are intelligent!

Make sure you listen, digest and meditate on the wisdom, and words you hear from those who have walked before you. Remember the pleas of your mother. You know what they are. Those I will always mean, even if I'm no longer here. Don't call it pressure. Stick to something, Don't change your mind like the weather.

You are too cool to argue. It's not worth it, is it? Procrastination will have you miss the progress ship. Watch how you blame others. That you will prosper greatly, is one of the prayers of your mother.

You can go as far as your passion will lead you. Lead, Lead, Lead. My seed! Handsome son of mine, you are a great man of God, follower of the Word, wise above your years, a creator and a striver.

Do your best and don't be afraid to push yourself. Don't hold it in. Let some steam off your chest and remember there is always a test.
Keep up the good work.

P.S. And you're not Zae!

Kenya Renee

Free Admission

AN ELDER'S VOICE

I would like to send this heartfelt letter to the youth of today. I'm hoping that something in this letter will get you to think about what direction your life is heading and how to reach your destiny. I want to start out with addressing this letter to the ladies.

Ladies, I have grown very tired of the things I have witnessed lately especially on Facebook and other social media sites. How can we expect guys and others to respect us when we don't even respect ourselves? God did not make you a bitch, thot or any other kind of derogatory name. When He created you, He made a queen to be revered and respected. Carry yourself in a respectable manner. A young lady should know that she doesn't have to parade around half naked to get a man's attention. Most men will tell you that you will never meet his mother if that's what you do. You don't have to be loud. You don't have to curse or be disrespectful to get attention at the mall, in stores, at school, or anywhere else. Get attention for being a good person and getting good grades. Excel in music or sports or volunteer at a nursing home or shelter. Get attention for being celibate or having high standards, morals, and integrity.

If you are a single mom, make your children a priority, not yourself. Once you have children, selfishness goes out the window. It's all about them now, not your hair, nails, shoes, and clothes. I'm not saying you can't look nice, but if you look good, so should your kids. And most important, never ever put a man before your child. Be careful who you bring around your children. Too many mothers are crying themselves to sleep because of their child being molested, raped, or murdered by someone they knew intimately. That child didn't ask to come here. You owe it to your child to be the best parent you can be and to protect them at all costs.

Young men, learn to respect yourselves as well so that society can respect you like the king you were created to be. Quit glorifying the thug image by sagging your pants and wearing excessive tattoos. I'm not interested in seeing what kind of underwear you have on today! Watch your tone and stop cursing around your kids and elderly people. And if you have kids, take care of them. No one should have to force you to take care of your own. Decide to be an exceptional father, regardless of whether you are with the mom. Build a lifelong relationship with your children and let them know that just because you are not in the home doesn't mean you don't love them. Try to be respectful to the mom and keep the peace so you can stay in contact with your children.

And finally, never let a woman take care of you. Do your part as men to take care of your family and responsibilities because if you don't, women will lose respect for you. Get a legal job so that you don't become a statistic like most—in jail or dead. You were created to be better than that.

Take pride in yourself, learn to speak proper English and be respectful. Slang is okay around your friends, but it won't get you a job. And every man should have at least one suit with dress shoes. You can't wear a white t-shirt, gym shoes, and jeans to a job interview. Be the type of man that you would want your sisters and mom to marry.

For both, finish your education. Graduate from high school and college and make something of yourself. It will help you find a better job, and you won't have to depend on anyone for your basic needs. Be careful of who you hang around. Trouble will always come with negative people. Avoid them at all costs. Last, but not least, put your trust in God. Find a suitable place of worship with a strong and solid foundation where you can receive the Word of God. It will help you grow and mature into a better person by showing you what to do when the troubles of this world come. Cultivating your spiritual grow will ensure that you will not do something negative that you will regret later. Forgive easily and love freely. Be the best person that you can be.

Sharon Payne

Valerie Winkfield

TEENAGE ME

Dear Teenage Me,

I write this letter to let you know that this is a pivotal time in your life! You have grown from a girl to a young lady. **With that transformation, some behaviors and thought processes need to change.** Stop seeking the wrong attention for the wrong reasons. A boy can never be a father figure because he has yet to mature into a man and gain all that comes with being a real man. So, don't look to him to meet your needs. Don't be surprised if he stands you up and dodges your phone calls. Don't take the "I love you's" seriously. That boy doesn't even know what love is, and you don't either. Trust me when I say that you'll have plenty of time for that. Life teaches you what love is, and you have not lived long enough. Look in the mirror right now, tell yourself, "I love you," and know that God loves you! Make it a daily habit for the rest of your life.

Love and embrace yourself no matter what your peers say. I know you keep hearing that you're too thin and that if you were just a little thicker the boys would like you. One day you'll miss being skinny. I know you keep hearing that your hair is too short, and it's too nappy. One day you and the world will appreciate your naturalness. Always keep your uniqueness to stand out from the crowd. Those who standout the most, shine the greatest. You will be surprised to know that the in-crowd ain't so popular ten years down the line. Everyone's path is different so stay on your own. It has already been laid out for you since the beginning of time.

If you feel as though your mom doesn't understand your struggles, talk to her anyway! She's your biggest supporter. Hiding your hurt will not make things better. Don't suffer in silence! Tell her what you're missing, even when you think she's not listening. Find a mentor in the adults around you—your teachers, church leaders, or neighbors. Let them know what your dreams and desires are. You'll be surprised at how much wisdom they have and their willingness to provide guidance.

Don't be afraid to have a voice. You are just as important as the next person.

> Never take any one's judgment of you to heart. Their opinions do not matter and they never will. Understand that they are trying to make up for what they lack. They see something in you that they don't see in themselves. You are smart, beautiful, and talented. If you want to be a writer, write until your fingers hurt and read everything you can. If you want to be a model, study the best. If you want to dance, move to the beats in your head. It is important that you put your interests first. Life is what you make it, no matter the setbacks, pain endured, or how much money you have. There are ways to cultivate your God-given gifts and talents. Let those skills be known to the world. There is a reason for them being special in your heart.

I know it's not easy being a teenager, and you're journeying through life on a bumpy road. Take the time to find enjoyment in not only the big things, but also the little things. I know you got teenage stuff on your mind, so you have to choose to think about the future because it's not far away. As you grow older, you'll experience how fast the days go by, when you have more fun things to do. Think about the college you want to attend, the career you want, and the place you want to live. Believe it or not, you can be doing things right now to work toward your future. You have a purpose. Wake up every day with one goal to accomplish, no matter how small or big. Setting goals are the building blocks for success.

Learn the importance of positivity because it will help

you get through your trials and tribulations.

Every dark side has a bright side. Even in the toughest situations, you will find that some good can come out of it. Nothing lasts forever, and the hard times are temporary. There is a reason for everything, even the things we don't understand. What does not kill you will make you resilient and strong enough to take on any challenge. It's alright to make mistakes but learning from them is the smartest thing you can do.

Love,

Future Me

Jor'Danna

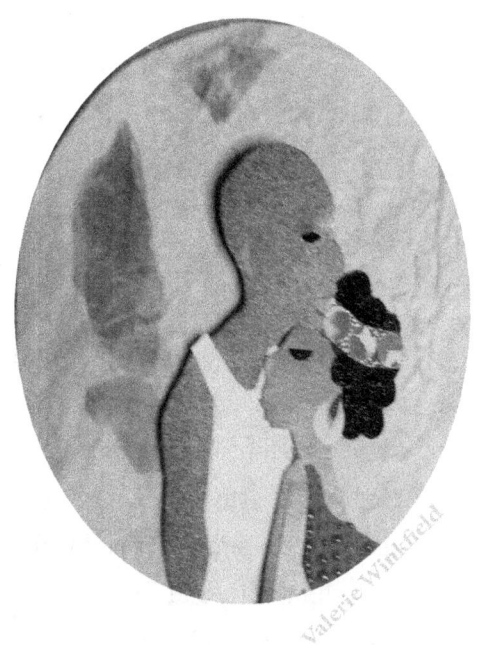

TO YEARS PAST

Dear Years Past,

It is not a common thing to write a letter as a means of contacting the past, especially in hopes of finding answers, providing warnings, or perhaps giving insight as to what's to come. However, it is this exception to the rule that I am privileged to contact you. I write this letter in the year of our Lord April 6, 2014. I don't know how far back this message will travel before it reaches the right person. If it lands in your hands and is read by your eyes, if you are not the right person, please let it continue through time.

We live in a blessed time with technology that has afforded us conveniences not even dreamed about 50 years ago. We have organized governments that mainly operate as a democracy, which professes to be for the people and by the people. We boast of religious freedoms, voting rights for all, with free and fair access to the judicial system. However, along with the blessings, governments and all of its systems, many questions arise regarding the problems we've experienced today as a result of failures within the system's operations. We question how we got to this point—to the point that excessive prisons are deemed unfair and there is economic disparity with significant unemployment in a land of such promise and wealth. It is your generation whose shoulders we stand on, whose plans we review.

Many people today ask the question, "What were you all thinking about and what were your expected outcomes?" Were these the results of operations within the system? We know that many things were out of your control as are many things out of our control today. However, with the things that you did control, what were your expected outcomes?

Am I talking to the right person? Please affirm in a loud voice, "I am the right person!"

I recently went to a human rights conference. The same issues were highlighted in 2014 that have been highlighted in years past, as far back as I can remember. The issues, such as torture at home and abroad in our prisons and military, are the same. Outrageous immoralities still exist. People are detained, for no reason, held captive without trial, and are sometimes assumed dead when they are alive. There are still issues with workers' rights, especially when it comes to fair and equitable wages. We are still concerned about workplace safety and corporate crime with greed. Crimes against women and women's rights are still major issues and are on the global stage along with religion. Civil rights and race discrimination are still agenda items that receive worldwide recognition. We've made some progress over the years in most of these areas. Tell me was it your plan to have these problems eradicated by this time? Many expect that we will eternally fight these causes. Did you know that? Would you have done anything different? If so, what? Many of these difficulties are comparable to other major topics, such as the war on drugs, which was supposedly not designed to be won. If you had known, would you have changed your approach?

Am I talking to the right person? Please affirm in a loud voice, "I am the right person!"

We also live in a time of environmental concerns that include toxic waste dumping, recycling, bioterrorism, pollution, and soil fertility, just to name a few. We criticize civilians for traveling between the states and in some cases abroad. We are made to believe that we've sinned in some way for traveling around the country and world. It's as though all of our freedom fighting was for naught.

We have popular commercials that announce, "You are now free to move around the country." The powers that be or vocals of our time are constantly boasting about some bigger picture out there that the rest of us are supposed to be sacrificing for or suffering to obtain. However, no one seems to know the bigger picture. We ask ourselves, "What's that about?" We ask quietly and in private. Some behave as though we are to stay in the same place all of our lives and never visit other cities, churches, countries, etc. Does that sound like the sort of freedom your generation fought to gain? We are concerned about the deliberate breakup of families, ethnic cleansing, family dysfunction, and displacements.

Our value system has changed in a negative way. These are some costs passed on to our generation. We are stuck with the bill. These are weeds planted in the lives of our children, who are being labeled and accused before they even get started. It is no wonder so many of us today are always asking why you think this about me or that about me, and so on. Could progress have continued without this type of destruction? Or, was this planned destruction? If so, who planned it? Were there other options?

Am I talking to the right person? Please affirm in a loud voice, "I am the right person!"

Paranoia and suspicion are common expressions of the time. Much of this behavior is the result of blatant government surveillance. It's not a secret anymore. Everyone in our society today is legally under review. Our phones are bugged. Mail is monitored and read. Internet and social media activity are observed. It is all done in the name of national security. Some label it political abuse, corporate abuse, or just say big brother (the government) is watching us all. We know that this behavior was predicted to come to pass in 1984. I suspect it was long before that time. How did your generation view this? You knew it was coming. Was there any stopping it? If so, what would you have done differently? How could we have been better prepared?

Am I talking to the right person? Please affirm in a loud voice, "I am the right person!"

Every period has its challenges. You had your victories. You fought your wars. We stand in this time, on your successes and failures. Many of the injustices your generation fought hard to end are resurfacing under another name. We still struggle to maintain freedom and independence at home and on the world stage. Tell me something about the times you lived in now. Would you keep it a secret, knowing that exposing it would have made a difference for the betterment of someone's life and maybe the world? Understanding a little more about time, would you tell it?

Am I talking to the right person? Please affirm in a loud voice, "I am the right person!"

Very Truly Yours,

Pamela S. B. Fagen
Voice of the Future
Chicago, IL,USA

AFIRMING, IN A LOUD VOICE,
              "I AM THE RIGHT PERSON!"

ADVICE FOR THE YOUTH

To My Dear Tenderonies,

I'm writing you this letter to express to you the **truth**. Yes, my truth. I'm hoping it will inspire you to go over and beyond what is expected of you. I'm writing you because this world is truly messed up. Please listen to what your elders have to say because that's wisdom that can prolong your life. Make sure you pray before going to bed each night. Promises are made to be broken. Watch the words spoken from your tongue. Know you're not the only one who has it rough. The streets are watching, so you have to be tough, and that I know. But some roads you just don't have to follow. You have choices, we all do. So think about that before you hang with your crew and fall into what they do.

The freaks come out at night. Remember that with success comes sacrifice. You can move a mountain. I know that may seem far-fetched, and keep those bible quotes etched in the front of your mind to keep you grounded, at least a majority of the time. Make sure you stand for something because weak minds fall for anything. Don't sell your soul for material things, like bling, because guess what? At the end of the day, those things won't mean a thing.

You must find peace, but you definitely won't find it hanging out in the streets 'cause it ain't no love in the heart of the city. Often times, what you see in the streets is not pretty, so soak up the game as it's taught to you. You don't have to do as they do. A hard head makes a soft butt. Do not cut class. Enjoy your youth while it lasts. Living a life that's fast can lead you straight to the penitentiary where you may spend your last and those jailbird peeps will be after your ass, literally!

Keep it positive. It's not cool to be a hell raiser. It's better to ask the Lord to be your Savior. I'm asking God to come save the youth. That's my truth. And I'm encouraging you to keep the faith. Slow and steady wins the race, and ask God to show you the way.

All the drinking will catch up, so keep your head up to the sky. Remember, just like Romeo, everyone must die. Ask yourself what's love without tragedy. There is so much in this big world for you to see. Expand your horizons and find someone close you can confide in confidently. Remember to say "Thank you" because no one owes you anything. Watch those one-night flings because they can cost you a lifetime.

In closing, remember to try and achieve your best. That means you must **never stop.** Keep learning and seek more knowledge. Don't get angry when people copy you by calling them haters. Remember that there is nobody greater than Him.

Kenya Renee

Free Admission

BRO BIGGER

All I have to be is halfway decent, due to his prior behavior.

In an instant, I become the average females' savior.

They observe my beanstalk of a pedestal as it grows.

I share my thoughts and choices at the crossroads.

Even with six different options,

my self-discipline shocks him

that I'm able to consolidate them.

The fork is now two.

Much respect due

to those big brothers who advise wisely.

Following his blueprint, I knew what my demise might be.

If dumb weren't so fun, we'd all make the left at that sign labeled

"No Trouble Here."

I shed my tears.

But he doesn't see me.

I'm busy leaving bread crumbs to rewrite his journey.

Wrong was right when it came to me.

If he said so.

My left was his right if it had to be.

If he said so.

Seven years my senior, he left at the right time.

Years of his guidance infiltrated my mind.

Full of twisted logic, I stroll and strut.

Chick after chick in the wind, jelly roll, and guts.

Mackadocious lines and street toned walk-a-bout.

No more, "Wassup Lil' (his name)," insert my own clout.

Right when I thought I could do no wrong he betrays me. I grieve.

For the next twenty years, left handedness is what he believes.

The weight of my righteousness is like a dangling planet.

The wrong amount of silence between brothers can strangle a granite.

He doesn't hear me cuss, but he feels the vibrato in his shoes.

The left and right hand is the wrong tug-of-war to resolve our issues.

Todd Parker

Free Admission

DEAR DAUGHTER

Daughter, I love you.

How wonderful it is to have a daughter like you. I'm proud of you. I constantly pray for you to be blessed in all you do. I'm inspired by the morals you possess and how you've grown to embrace "your" differences. You stand above many others in your own right.

You're my best friend, the one I gossip with all of the time. I hope we know each other when our next lives begin. You will win! In all that you do! I certainly pray that you do! Remember the words of wisdom from me to you. Please hold to heart all that our family has been through, my little Kenya #2.

Hoping you will follow in some but not all of my footsteps. Strive for the best and don't give up! Know that it's okay just to be quiet when it's time. Learn to not give a f**k about petty things, and you'll be just fine.

Don't get mad, get better. Your young adult years have just begun. Don't cry long about losing a man because you can always get another one, and another one and another one.

Get the most of each step you make. Remember what I taught you, and pray to the Lord each night for your soul to take.

You were born with audacity. A great fine woman, you've grown up to be. Don't second guess your feelings and don't beat yourself up.

As you know, friends come and go. Life is not over once you become a parent. And as a mother and wife you will make mistakes.

I can never run out of words to say about you because my praise is never ending. I may not have given you a hug today but know that I love you.

Kenya Renee

Admit 6
Celebrating Kizzy

- My Friend, My Soul Mate, Katerria 'Starr' Doty *100*
- Ripples, Todd Parker *102*
- An Aura Of Strength, Sharon Payne *105*
- A Warriorette, Kenya Renee *107*
- Moments Of Encouragement, Jor'Danna *109*
- Faith • Love • Courage, Pamela S. B. Fagen *110*
- Black To Blue Heaven, Schreece Jones *112*

KIZZY'S LEGACY

- Blues, *114*
- Jesus Loves Me, *115*
- Thank You, *116*

MY FRIEND, MY SOUL MATE

When I picked up the phone and dialed your cell phone number to speak to you, my friend and soul mate, I heard this lady say, **"The subscriber you have dialed is not in service. If you feel, you have reached this message in error, please hang up and try your call again later."**

Here I am alone, without you. I'm faced with all these life changing events, and no longer can we converse, put our heads together and come up with a plan, encourage one another, or cheer for one another. Even as adults we accepted each others temper tantrums, when things didn't go our way. And when it was all said and done, we still loved each other.

No one can do that for me now, I thought as I sat out in the yard that we created with you in mind while our daughters laughed. Our common denominator is no longer with us—you! We're trying to move forward. I mean all of us: your husband, children, family, and friends.

So now we meet up in memory of you, but I cry at night because I'd much rather have you! I cried last night, hell I cry. I cry because I grew tired and worn mentally as I witnessed your health decline so rapidly. You told me, as you looked me in the eyes, "Boo I'm going to die from this. Nothing they can do." I heard you. I know we talked about the day. However, I cried because you wanted us to go on with our lives without you, but I would not entertain that conversation with you. It is our God that I depended on to do what I wanted Him to do. Truthfully, it didn't hit me until we went to your house on a Sunday evening, April 27th. I saw you in so much pain, lying in the bed. I cried because I realized just how selfish I'd been concerning you. My prayers were to keep you to see Parisha off to her prom, and even through her graduation.

It was then that I walked as if lightening were chasing me to the bathroom, to release tears due to my final decision. My decision was to release you, let go, and let God. That was when I realized time was no longer on our side. I was guilty of wanting some of you rather than to lose all of you! I cried last night. I may cry tonight because now that you're gone, I see just how amazing you were. I appreciate you. I cry when I remember the conversation we shared, when you told me you finally "get me." You told me how happy you were with my evolving into the woman I am!

I cry Kizzy because it was at the end that you realized why I live this carefree life. I understand why the caged bird sings! I know you are free. You showed us at your wedding anniversary that you appreciated life. I read your writing to your husband, family, and friends, as you instructed me to do. Boo, they were in awe. But not really, because the spirit led you to write those things, and they were appropriate for that day and time. That was a great sign to let us all know you are free.

I cried last night because there are some areas we didn't discuss, and now I wish I had asked you, just how you wanted them handled. I didn't. So now, I try tuning into your spirit so I can hear from you!

Dear Kizzy,

In my mind we had so much unfinished business…I love you.

Katerria "Starr" Doty

RIPPLES

The water is easy and free. At least today it is. But, of course, it's not always this way. There are days in which it can be busy with its body language. It speaks of the past with descriptive lingo. Its flow can say so much within minutes and leave a meaningful, lasting impression. A ripple. Many, many ripples. Like she did. Despite knowing her for only such a short time.

The **ripples** that remained after she blessed the ground with her essence were distinct. Look out for that canoe. Here comes a massive one that no one thinks they can avoid. But only she realizes that this behemoth will not interrupt her distinguished **ripples**. They come in the form of offspring that will spread her vivacious spirit for so many years to come. She spoke with a speed as if there was a tide quickly approaching. That tide was carrying the amount of stress that would envelop the average port city in one pass.

However, she transformed the most intimidating tidal wave into the calmest **ripples** with just a smile. There are large ones, and there are small ones. Some are in rhythmic conjunction with the wind that tap dances across the neighboring grass. It's as if they are in natural sync with one another. She was in sync with mother earth and all of her humble cubs. And as most cubs are when mother is nearby, they are mesmerized by the **ripples** of the omnipotent body of water.

They attempt to duplicate the encompassing **ripples** by attacking the eastbound stream. Yet, the effect of their interruption doesn't equate the pause she puts into everyone's heart and mind. Her outlook on life, the life she grasps, the life she cherishes, and the life she leads making others appreciate their lives, are phenomenal. Our encounters were minimal, but little does she know that I learned from her as we interacted. Bad days aren't as bad since we met. Road rage decreased. Work didn't seem like work.

Relationships were strengthened. The sun shined brighter. The moon's glow was lighter. Stars let it be known that we are all just a couple of sugar lumps inside your least favorite company appreciation mug.

We are trying to stretch every nanosecond out of this coffee break called life. She taps the mug with her heavenly insight and creates more **ripples**. She leaves her indentation everywhere she goes. Her laughter trickles into the depths of every listener's inner listener. We all realize her soon-to-be, and we cringe. At least the most of us. Definitely one of us. Yet, she basks in the absolution that she has paved the path for others who seek the true expression of what it means to live life to the fullest. Each and every day. **Ripples**. Each and every day. We do our best at extending coffee breaks as long as we possibly can. Even at the expense of being late, draped with excuses, we need that coffee. Well, she knew it was short in time, but attempted to pack it with all the knowledge that she possessed.

Later for the singular undertone and inspirational edge, let the woman leave her **ripples** the way she desired. If you look closely, you can still witness them make their way through your town, and your town, and your town. You'll double take like most. Of course, every person has a reason to grace Earth with their presence. The majority of us can only hope to figure out that reason before the coffee becomes room temperature. More importantly, before something takes place that would warrant us to seek that reason immediately. Coffee shot. And then there are those that can maximize their entire coffee break by leaving a bit in a cup for the next person to view the **ripples**. I was motivated by her leaving her cup o' **ripples** behind for all to peer. By doing this, she boldly blended things we take for granted into the **ripples** we should never undermine—Seize one.

I can't help but to remember her from the first joke she unknowingly recited all the way to the event of her home-going. The same event will always dictate instructions within life. And that is, to take advantage, full advantage, of your coffee break. The six-block parade of representation on that fateful Saturday is indicative of how much positivity she was responsible for in this life.

Free Admission

There are some words, in certain rhythms and arrangements, that move us, sometimes on a daily basis. We look forward to those affirmations on a daily basis. Take a look at the next set of **ripples** that you witness. A puddle. Cup of coffee. Teardrops. The laughter of a child.

Hey Kizzy.

Todd Parker

AN AURA OF STRENGTH

I remember the first time I met Kizzy. She sat next to me at Adrienne's home. I looked her over. She had an aura about her, sweet, innocent and young. She seemed kind of timid and quiet to me at first. I noticed that she had small hands, and I smiled, not really knowing why. All I knew about her was that she was our leader Starr's best friend. When she began to speak and tell her story, the woman I looked upon as weak became strong. She testified about her struggles with her health and the second bout with cancer. She shared the trials she endured the first time the cancer occurred and she promised to fight off the disease just as she did before. In spite of what was taking place in her body at the time. After I heard her plight, I began to look at her differently.

She was no longer a fragile young lady but a strong, beautiful woman who was so full of life. As she shared her story with us, tears began to well up in my eyes. I couldn't believe her willingness to share the ups and downs of chemo and the damage it had done to her body as it returned once again. She told stories of doctor visits and how emergency room moments unfolded. I had no right to cry, not if she wasn't going to.

So, I sat there in awe, admiring this petite lady who had so much to live for giving us all she had to give with her words. As she talked, she pulled us in making us wish that her life could be different. She had a husband and kids who adored her. I wondered how they felt letting her come here to share her stories. Was it too much for them?

I remember Adrienne calling to say that Kizzy was ill and in the hospital. She stated that it would be days now and there was nothing they could do but make her as comfortable as possible. I began to cry. I was still reeling from my own dad's passing, and ill feelings of another loved one leaving surfaced once again.

I didn't know what to say except that I would pray for her and her family. I

Free Admission

thought about the family she was leaving behind and how they would miss her. How would the girls continue on without their mother in their last year of high school? There were proms to attend, graduations to get ready for, and I'm sure much more. I was concerned about her husband and how overwhelmed he must be with reliving this twice, hoping and praying that it would have a positive end.

Weeks later, Kizzy passed away peacefully. I remember feeling numb when I received the call. I pushed myself to say something, anything about the loss we all felt. It didn't seem fair that such a beautiful person was taken from this earth, but I had to trust God with His decision.

At the meetings, her presence was missed. Sometimes if I close my eyes real tight, I can see her sitting to the left of me smiling and looking like she didn't have a care in the world. I miss you Kizzy. Rest in peace.

Sharon Payne

A WARRIORETTE

Hey girlie. I'm so glad we met. Thank you for all the inspirational words you shared with me.

I've looked at how you raised the girls and how they are your world. Mrs. Fast Talker, you are something else. Funny, 'cause I can't compare you to anyone else. Some might say, "Kizzy, that girl is crazy." I look at you as such a lady. I look back to the day that you first mentored me. **You gave me such good relationship advice. If I can just remind myself of the advice you gave: "You can keep the man you love forever happy in your life with spice."**

Wow, we lost a good lady to the dreadful Big "C" that has tainted our society. You continue to care about life and the ones you love, looking upon all of us from the heavens above. Even in the middle of your situation, you used words as an elevation. You built a solid foundation for others to follow. Not having you here with us is most definitely a tough pill to swallow. Our hearts will forever be touched and filled with your joyous smile, a mothers' smile, a sisterly smile. I miss your smile. But when I think of your smile, I smile.

Hey girlie, thank you for showing me the characteristics of a warriorette, full of womanly etiquette, unforgettable like the memory of an elephant. Your legacy will continue forever. Indefinite!

Wow, it's been a few months now. Awareness is what I hear on the television and radio. We see all those pink bows, but where does the funds go? How do we find a cure? No one knows. I must stop my rant now before these tears soak my clothes. "Be strong my friend" is what you'd tell me, Kizzy. I know!

There were some things you had to endure, but you were never lost in your

Free Admission

struggle.

When I think of our moments, I choose to smile and it is followed by heavy chuckles. Your love language for me, I can never muffle. Here are just a few words I use to describe you: Wife, mother, provider, counselor, cook, teacher, confidant, and motivator.

Kizzy Boo,

Kenya Renee

MOMENTS OF ENCOURAGEMENT

Dear Kizzy,

Though we had a brief acquaintance, I learned a lot from getting to know you. During our icebreaker discussion at the first P.O.P Writer's meeting, you revealed to me that you were fighting for your life. I must admit that I was surprised because you were in such high spirits, your personality was so vibrant and warm. Your words of encouragement made me feel good about the steps that I was taking in my life. It was as though you sensed my doubt and uncertainty about those steps.

I remember telling you that I was working on finishing up my second graduate degree. You commented on how inspiring it was to go to the next level. You told me not to let anyone keep me from pursuing what I wanted to do in life. Little did you know that I had my share of nay-sayers. I will never forget how much you emphasized being true to ourselves and being vulnerable because our story can touch and inspire others. Considering the fact that I am a reserved person, your remarks really served as a guide for me while writing my pieces. After all, we have our "stuff" and no one's life is flawless. Although you are not here in the flesh, I am confident that you are continuing to inspire, encourage, and uplift in the spirit.

Love,

Jor'Danna

FAITH • LOVE • COURAGE

Dear Kizzy,

I knew you for a brief time. The time was brief but the memories are lasting. You gave free admission into your present struggles. Our paths crossed at two P.O.P Writers meetings. The first meeting of our group and the first meeting at your best friend's house.

My first impression of you was courage. I found you to exhibit such strength. We all knew then that you were dealing with a life-threatening disease. You appeared to be handling it well. My second impression of you was faithful. You had such trust in God. You verbalized your faith and belief that God would see you through this and that it was going to be good. My third impression of you was caring. You displayed concern about others in the midst of your own personal pain and struggles. My fourth and most lasting impression of you was messenger. The conversation we had after the meeting at your best friend's house was lasting. I gave you a ride home, and you gave me encouragement and a message. In summary, I saw you as a messenger of **faith, love, and courage.** Your spirit is eternal, and it appears that God has lifted you to another level of consciousness.

Kizzy, you've made your transition. You have made it to the other side. You are on your way home. You prepared for your children and your husband whom you left behind. Everyone that spoke on your behalf at your home going commented on the instructions you left for the care of your girls and support for your husband. You are truly a Proverbs woman. You paved the way and paid the price for your daughters' security. I am so happy I met you while you were on this side of life. I wish you a good afterlife.

Your journey to the heavens should be sweet. I believe the Creator has a job for you during your heavenly journey. It's so obvious, now that you've transitioned. You are close to creation now, with a spiritual reach that you couldn't experience before. You saw something in this life. You knew something, and experienced something that you can now address on a spiritual level. There is nothing that can defeat you now, because God is with you.

You have taught me and so many others what it means to have **faith**, **love**, and **courage**. Your spiritual message in the after life will certainly be one to acknowledge. I believe you have unfinished business. When I look to the clouds, I know you'll be there. Have a pleasant but purpose filled journey.

Sincerely,

Pamela S.B. Fagen
A brief acquaintance

BACK TO BLUE HEAVEN

4-28 will remain in my mind until I cease to be.
The day God allowed me to be born into this world the day he took my dear friend into eternity.
It amazes me how he knew at the beginning of creation that we would share
a day,
a time,
place,
space.
My beginning, our ending.
Her beginning.
She went back to Blue Home.
I must admit I was selfish,
didn't want you to depart,
yet in the logical parts
of my mind and the
trust, hope, and faith inside my heart
I understand that there is
always a plan.

Our God makes no mistakes.
I never considered finding you
after so many years
and you slipping away in
a breath,
heartbeat,
moment,
blink of an eye,
mere seconds,
or less,
Time
is relative,
I guess.
Precious,
I know
you were sick,
yet
I never thought
you would die.
It never entered
or crossed my mind.
I never considered
your spirits

needed to depart
the beautiful vessel
God allowed it to dwell in.
Yet you were fragile,
as we all are.
I still have your smile
when I close my eyes,
I can still hear your last voice mail
Playback in my mind
I can hear you say
"I Love You Girl."
It amazes me how we live
parallel and apart.
Got the same wedding ring,
Wedding colors too (blue),
yet during that time we were
worlds apart from each other.
I will cherish the time that we spent
remembering that day
I came to your house
just to hang out.
We talked, caught up.
About five minutes in you said,
"I hope you're okay, but this scarf has
to come off."

I said it was fine
because I had my encounter with
cancer,
so I know what it means.
My Mom is still surviving!!
So we sat,
me with my extremely large bundles of
joy inside
and you with the only visible sign of
your illness,
that beautiful, smooth, bald head,
looking at our wedding photos,
flipping through magazines
with our blue footies on,
laughing and talking
until we were tired.
Then I lay on my couch, you on yours,
and watched you sleep.
I am so grateful
that God allowed me to spend time
with you
before you did what we all must do:
go back, back to blue,
go back, back to blue.

Schreece Jones

Free Admission

KIZZY'S LEGACY

BLUES

Blue is my favorite color.
Sometimes I feel blue
but not only on Monday mornings.
The color blue can pattern my life.
I have had turns and bumps
and always found myself back to
cool blue.
Blue comes in some of the prettiest
shades,
and people may view it as dark,
yet, it is light when it shows up
in the sky.
You see peace and calmness in the
water at the beach,
and you can dive deep in the
reflection of blue.
Blue always comforts my mind
and drenches me in its tranquility.
It brings purpose and defines who
I am and what I want from my life.
Blue is belief, love,
understanding—that's me.
The part of my life
I want people to review
is the honest, devoted, passionate
true blue.

JESUS LOVES ME

JESUS LOVES ME,

THIS I KNOW.

For the Bible tells me so...
So I asked my God why?
Why am I here again?
He told me to stay put
and He shall show.
Oh and God came
and He showed up and out!
Yes, took my breast,
not one but both.
Took all of my lymph nodes
and through my doctor said,
  "You're cancer free."

JESUS LOVES ME,

THIS I KNOW.

I praised Him and thanked Him
for saving my life!
I couldn't wait to tell
everybody what my God did for me.
Stop!

KNOCK!
KNOCK!

"Who's there?"
"Cancer.
          I'm back!"
WHO?"
"WHAT DO YOU MEAN?

I fell to my knees
and cried to my God,
  "I thought you cured me!"

My God said, "I did, but I need you to finish letting my children know to continue to have faith in me. The only way they will know is when they see my work in you."

The tears dropped like rain, falling from the sky.
"I give myself and lean to you my God."

YES, JESUS LOVES ME.

YES, JESUS LOVES ME.

Free Admission

THANK YOU

Dear God,

I want to say thank you!

I want to say thank you for all you have given me.

I want to say thank you for my life, my family, and my friends.

Thank you for all the many blessings and for covering me.

THANK YOU

I want to thank each and every person in this room.
I also want to thank the ones that are not here, that supported me. Everybody warms my heart because I'm still here.
But today really warms my heart because of my family and friends that are here. I thought giving birth was really hard, but I must say going through Cancer was the toughest.
I thought I was alone. I thank God, and celebrate, and most of you all see my smiles again,

KIZZY GIVENS 1977—2014

Admit 7

Love Jones

- **Habit Forming**, Todd Parker *118*
- **My Love**, Kenya Renee *122*
- **Chris**, Sharon Payne *124*
- **Jonesin'**, Pamela S.B. Fagen *126*
- **A Complex Attraction**, Jor'Danna Davis *128*

Free Admission

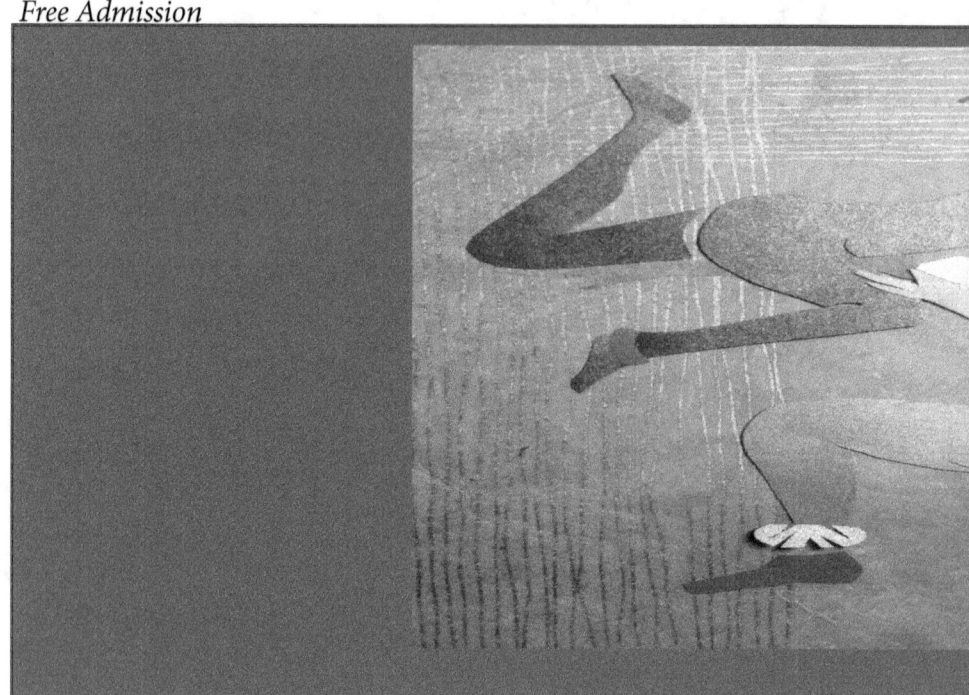

HABIT FORMING

I had a love once or twice. I'm a
master's-degreed individual.
Over-underrated vocab for the
boardroom and the poker table.
But that Jones defined irrationality and
a complex mentality.
Shame on reality.
For showing me my first, my true, and
my forbidden love inside the same circle
of my discovery.
At first love, you miss your
togetherness, that so-called
forever-ness.
hoping it doesn't end because you'd miss
her very existence.

Never knew music meant so much
when you're not even listening.
It's a short drive.
But love truly is stronger than anyone's
pride.
Damn you Sade.
I did my first
so wrong as a youngster.
Sought forgiveness beyond
my novice days.
Struggled inside my conflicted haze
as I revealed the future man in me.
and I paid dearly; yearly.
She amplified her role as my first lady
upon the foreground of MJB.
The sound track of our discovery. The
implant of we,
into each other's families.

Access to the Soul

Valerie Winkfield

I look good in blue,
but her favorite was green,
so I rep teal on a regular basis.
Face it.
She even taught you how to
drive a stick.
There was no denying her input
to my manhood,
as if she and my pops sat together
to discuss it.
The plan was to be a player like society
promotes a man to do.
What it fails to show you
is how to remain manly as you
buckle in her arms,
fall victim to her charms, and tip-toe
around her friends hen circle.
Did more than a few
to be the man for the love
that was meant to be true.
I grew up, hung up, and blew up
my flimsy love parameters.
The list I recorded promising myself,
and my boys,
of what I would never do,
due to my true love's hoodoo,
was soon cat box material.
The daydreams of her kept my
soul-stice in a state of completeness.
I was her cheerleader,
and I kept the f***ing uniform.
She became my heart's
personal psychologist.
Even though it seems biased.
She made me jones
even more for her.

P.O.P Writers 119

Free Admission

It became unfair for future others.
What do you do
when the love you've experienced
envelops you?
You celebrate it with the same pressure
per inch
as her clutch made.
You respond sensitively, yeah babe.
I wanted every lady after her to possess
the same quirks,
but that never worked.
A playful tap to my head
as she walks by,
or freeing her inner-brat on the fly.
Respecting her wishes
to be her own woman without me.
Yeah babe. Wait, no,
well, yeah babe.
Love is becoming a new rules maker by
the day.
My future baby gyrl has to discover my
erogenous zones without my writing it
down. Yeah babe.
I can't explain it,
and there's no inner force helping me
to disclaim it.
She defames my declaration for her
heart, drives off in my car,
leaves me to hold baggage,
and says she'd have a better time
without me.
Pass the glass, Mr. Jones.
I'll be here when she
blows right by me.
Ms. Forbidden split my diameter into
three radii.
One for the sense
we made together,

Access to the Soul

one for the sense it made to be apart,
and one for the bio reaction
I experience as I write this.
Everlasting bliss as I reminisce about
this miss.
She defined forbidden,
as an older vixen.
That backdrop made for a
delectable taboo.
Volatile.
In the most tolerable manner.
Upheaval.
In the most believable manner.
Sexual.
In the most infect-you-al manner.
Could swear I didn't drive past her
house waiting for her to peek.
I sneak.

Could swear I promised not
to feel this way.
I sway.
Could swear I could handle her so she
wouldn't roam.
I clone.
Now that's a
Jameson/Jones/Johnson
for us all.
Get with this while I am a man.
You can forget about ever proving you're
a wiser man.
You can say it.
I've said it.
But only a Joneser will admit it.
That there was a time when they never
knew the letter J existed.

Todd Parker

MY LOVE

My Love, as I look at you, my mind wonders.
I'm happy now—no longer in a sorrow slumber.
You found me.
My soul mate, I think back to the first day we met.
I was in line and you were the boss. It was meant to be,
this marriage between you and me.
When I'm around you, I feel like dancing.
You get me with your sincere romancing. It's my mind you enhance.
Now I finally have the chance to give **love** back.
You love me for me. You know the real definition of monogamy.
You who come home to me every night, my good luck charm causing no harm. You make my body shiver with those great words you deliver.
You mean them in every way.
An irresistible man, trying to do the best he can.
I know I must understand.
You exhibit many traits,
working hard with those strong, irresistible hands.
Happy you, are my man.
Syrupy sweet, I can sop you up from your head to your feet.
My eyes gleamed when we joined as a team—all others we out-beat.
I'm the winner. You are my ace of spades.
Together we will travel until a ripe old age.
Our book is full of chapters, you are the director, I am the actor.
You set me free to rapture to the next stage.

Kenya Renee

Adrienne Bruce

CHRIS

Like a moth to a flame,
our love can't be denied.
It's much too strong
to give up the ride.

It makes me act foolish,
in rhymes and in seasons.
It makes me break out
of my normal reasons.

I try to let it go,
but it keeps me intact.
I try to run away,
but I keep coming back.

I love when you speak,
I trust your thoughts.
Please share your dreams
and the memories
you've caught.

I want to hear your secrets
I promise not to share.
I'll keep them in my heart
in perfect gentle care.

And, as I watch you
from across the room

that million dollar smile
erases all gloom.

He doesn't understand
why I love him so much.
And he'll never understand
the joy of his touch.

My heart's in his pocket.
My V is on locket.
This loving he's cocking
and damn, I can't stop it!

Those strong, manly hands,
that chest all aglow,
he's turning me on
I wonder if he knows.

Those soft lips I need.
Those teeth so white
Can't wait til you kiss me.
I need you tonight.

I try to act cool,
but my body's on fire!
If you look in my eyes
you'll see my desire.

So I'm waiting on you...

Sharon Payne

JONESIN'

Come let me share my experience with you. About that amazing chemistry that makes you weak in the knees. Those beliefs get you obsessed with loving thoughts that overwhelm your entire head.

I'm talking about jonesin'.

I become instantly affected by personality, emotions, mind, and physical chemistry. I know when it's there. It's like a magnet pulling me. I feel curious, aroused, puzzled, and outright ambitious. Suddenly the sensuality in me is awakened. I've lost all sense of reservation. I now desire to be satisfied not only sexually, but also I require fulfillment in body, mind, and spirit.

I'm jonesin'.

There I was at home, on a nothing-special kind of night, relaxing and surfing the channels. Finally, I find something worth watching or something worth watching me. I was a little bit tired and not exactly focused on the program, floating between awake and asleep. As I doze, some of those old sensations resurfaced, and I began to feel aroused. It seemed that someone engaged me in foreplay. I instantly became alert. I looked around me, just to make sure everything was okay. I poured myself a glass of wine and started to sip. Once more, in my mind I still felt stimulated to a degree of sexual arousal.

I'm jonesin'.

I wish to have a sexual escapade. I miss that warm and fuzzy feeling on the inside. I long to have that girlish giggle that comes from pure innocence and excitement. I crave to feel attended to, desired, and wanted. I need to be remembered on holidays and all special occasions, both public settings and those privately created just for lovers. I require that intimate touch that could only be stimulated by passion.

Is this what I'm remembering, or is this what I'm sensing. I'm relaxed and continue to feel this foreplay, the caressing of my genitals, and then the in and out penetration of my vagina. Wow! It feels so good I don't want it to end. I jump to my feet, knowing that this can't be real because there's nobody in the bed with me. I thought I must be hallucinating. It's been so long since I've been with a man in this capacity that maybe I have a real live **Jones** going on.

I wanted it and whatever I was seeking was also seeking me. My sexual desires pursued me like a stalker in the night. I could feel the in and out, yes! Yes! I could. The in and the out was so real I was throbbing inside. Again, I sprang to my feet in fear that I was experiencing some kind of supernatural encounter. My genitals felt tender. Was this real or imagined? There was a feeling of lovemaking on my body, I felt sexed, but no one was there with me.

It was just some real jonesin' goin' on.

Directly after that experience, I had to reflect on it. I thought to myself, when I give love, I want the receiver to be there with me and know that I'm an equal and willing participant. There is nothing wrong with hot sex between two consenting adults. When I give love, I want my companion to know that I remember what's important to him. My partner has to know me. I want my man to listen to my body language of love. Touch me here, touch me there, kiss me, hug me, and rub me until I melt. Come out of hiding. I want to call you into existence with my attentiveness to you as well. I will make you feel wanted and loved to the highest degree.

I'm jonesin' for that loving relationship with a significant other.

Pamela S.B. Fagen

A COMPLEX ATTRACTION

Mist in the air from the water in which I bathe surrounds me
Mirrors become foggy,
and the steam from the bathroom walls began to drip
My eyes grow heavy, and my mind starts to drift
It was a month ago when I saw him for the first time
and committed a victimless crime
While running on nature's path,
I struggled to inhale the spring air as he ran past me
Muscles bulging from every part of his chocolate towering frame
Exchanging quick glances with my heartbeat dancing
Oh, these wild thoughts I had to tame
It was such a complex attraction, our souls so magnetic
Introductions were made, and numbers exchanged
Excitement was alive in my core and these feelings I could not ignore
Picking up the phone, I dialed the number to tonight's destiny
We both wanted each other's company, so our souls were in agreement
Hours later, I'm dwelling in a secret place shut off to the world
As he grips my body, my heart plummets to my stomach
The rain pounds on the roof of our love nest
and I swear it drops to the beat of his love within me
Bodies intertwined ever so gently like a python squeezing its prey
You see, it was a victimless crime, and I am about to commit foul play

Access to the Soul

Mouths quivering, knees shaking and bodies shivering

A complex attraction, oh this complex reaction

I am now a fanatic, and he's got all of the control

Weakness consumes me, and I become limp,

almost lifeless

Spooning in silence,

I'm wondering if this will be just a sweet memory or my true reality

Maybe he is Adam, and I am his Eve

because I am bound to become his rib

How could I have caught a love jones so quick?

Oooo wee…this time,

I've really got myself in a bind, man I'm really in the thick

Never to escape this tight hold he has on me

Although, things are not always what they seem,

I dare not let this be a mere dream.

I could endlessly ponder about what could be,

but for now I will live in the moment.

I'm left wide open with this complex attraction so potent.

Jor'Danna

Admit

8

Blended Family

- Fruitful & Multiplied, Sharon Payne *132*
- Encountering Challenge, Kenya Renee *133*
- Interpretation of Family, Pamela S.B. Fagen *135*
- A Beautiful Blend, Pamela S. B. Fagen *137*
- Life Lessons, Jor'Danna Davis *138*

FRUITFUL & MULTIPLIED

I must say that a blended family is something I truly know about in detail. You see, I am the oldest of my siblings of my biological mother and stepfather's children. My stepfather had one son, Willie Douglas Jr., before he married my mom. And because of their union, I was blessed to have three more siblings, Marcuse, Mervyn, and Jackie.

I grew up with these siblings in every normal fashion possible, never using the words half or step. We were one, and that was all that mattered. But, I also knew that another family of mine existed through my biological father, Robert Wilson II. He had 28 children altogether, with one being deceased. This news was brought to light at his funeral where I met many of my sisters and brothers for the first time. I felt out of place, almost as if I didn't really belong. Some looked like me and smiled like me, but I didn't feel the connection. I only knew some of them as I was growing up. I recognized Bobby, Terrance, Gregory, Ricky, Tito, Curtis, Rolando, Rolnita, and Tikki (Byron), but the rest were a mystery to me. I'm sure they felt the same. I have tried to reach out to some of them on Facebook. They've been nice and cordial, but it's still kind of weird to know you share a bloodline with someone and not really know that person.

Well, I guess all you can do is start anew and get to know them. We often laugh amongst ourselves because of this poem my dad wanted included in his obituary. It simply says, "The Bible said 'be fruitful and multiply.' I did my part, and that's no lie!" Boy, I think that says it all.

Sharon Payne

ENCOUNTERING CHALLENGE

Things understood need not be said. But that depends on who says it and how it's understood. I warn my friends and others who have never experienced it. AVOID, IF POSSIBLE, the strain of blended families. I hear their quoted replies, "It's hard finding a mate without children already, at my age."

What I will say may not be pretty to some but understand that I can't please everyone. A unique challenge each will encounter. Assuming a similar role from the former one expects. ENFORCE THE NO DISRESPECT RULE! From the steps because children will try it. Others hope for a split, but that's not shit. You may have to deal with the ex-Bitch!

Am I angry, no! Just letting you know how far some will go. I'm speaking from experience, and that's what taught me. My eyes have seen it multiple times in my household throughout my dating world. First off, I have two children who witnessed a split up of parents, who shared their existence with children of others for brief moments in their lives. And I'm pretty sure some of them run across their minds from time to time.

Conflict and resolution are the solutions when you're handed someone else's obligations, and they become your chore. Make your standards plain and simple or one of you could be looking at the front door. A combination of families to care for is what's in store. Arguments and strife abide every time they are there. It feels like you're at war.

If you've done it once and it's not for you, JUST DON'T DO IT ANYMORE! Stay aligned with the FAMILY RULES and all should be fine. But watch for the signs, they will undermine, because remember they don't have your same bloodline. Don't get me wrong, things can change for the better because, truthfully, success comes when you strive for a healthy family relationship that will last a lifetime. Within each family, sometimes there are favorite picks, so imagine how extended family members can throw tricks all up in your mix. Things can get quite messy, so put an end to ANY bull crap in your house really quick.

No matter what you do, just know they may not listen to you. The children determine whether they will like you. But let them know you're not trying to take their parents' spot. Tame the fire because things can get extremely hot. Bringing drama in your house, let it be known, in your home—NOT!

The first was like apples. The second is like pears, so remember and talk to them so they don't compare. Encourage them to be fair so that there will be clear air, or they just won't be allowed over there.

It's important to know everyone's role. Respect for adults should be understood because we are the ones in control of our homes. Strengthen the connection. Interests you must discover to find a common ground. Children may feel lost, but with your guidance, they can be found.

Choose to live happily as a unit, not separately. Remember, an immediate loving situation will not happen overnight. Unhappiness in your house is not worth the fight. Bottom line: We have the power to keep our families tight. One last thing, don't forget to pray each and every night.

Kenya Renee

INTERPRETATION OF FAMILY

A blended family to me means a mixing of various characters and concepts. It is a process similar to blending ingredients together to make a smoothie. Sometimes this is not easy because blending means combining methods and thoughts that may not bring about cohesiveness and this could be dangerous.

Biological families were merged from birth. It didn't cost anything to become a member, birth ensured the right to enter, and the members are a part of the same genealogical tree. That lineage could be one of race, values, country, culture, inheritance, etc. The common denominator here is that it wasn't a choice, and the members had nothing to do with entering. Most families are made this way, and that could be a great thing or maybe not. Biological blending is not your choice. You got a free ticket into this blend.

Extended families are made by merging the biological characteristics of others beyond the main family nucleus. An example of this is when a married couple welcomes an adoptive child from outside of the family nucleus. An example of this could be when a married couple who welcomes the union of an adoptive child from someone outside of the family nucleus. This union allows a child from a different bloodline to now share the bloodline of another family. The child has both families to call his or her own.

Many families come together by other means. We have community families, work families, career families, friendship families, church families, adopted families, political families, social families, and special interest families of all types. The common denominator here is the same belief, value, profession, business, community, etc.

In other words, there is a bond that extends beyond the blood line. Even though the commonality is not blood, the bond is just as thick, and in many cases, thicker. This is my interpretation of family.

THE STORY

The Extended Family is the main character.
Traditional families live their lives based on a concept that is connected only by blood. However, Traditional Family wanted to extend this concept by connecting with values, tradition, history, friends, career, churches, and special interest organizations.

Extended Family came into existence and looked at all the connections it obtained and thought this is good. Very good! Extended Family thought, why not extend this concept further? Extended Family immediately went to work to connect all that in the entire world. It wanted to add countries, all people, animals, and different values and customs. Extended Family was successful in achieving this and is now everywhere, and it has created a worldwide concept.

EnJay Photography

A BEAUTIFUL BLEND

He took some people unmatched by blood.
It was God's choice, and there was no flood.
Only the common ground of spiritual union,
and it caused a rare transfusion.
The start of a worldwide trend.

WHAT A BEAUTIFUL BLEND

The people came from all over in churches, communities, and careers.
They shared beliefs, values, organization, and history for many years.
They championed many causes, and they deserve our cheers.
Because where there's no division, only togetherness appears.
Building lifelong friends

WHAT A BEAUTIFUL BLEND

He heard a cry from country and people, who wanted to understand,
how to connect their hands.
Now they extend across the sands to many lands,
and the world can follow the Master's plan.
joining Nations as families and kin.

OH, WHAT A BEAUTIFUL BLEND!

Pamela S. B. Fagen

LIFE LESSONS

A while ago, mom remarried, and three other siblings came with the package. Since I was already an adult, I never imagined I could be an influence on my new stepsisters and stepbrothers. I thought, especially since our parents are different and we weren't raised together, that this new situation would be difficult. Additionally, I practically raised my biological sister and being protective of the intricate relationship that we share, brought some resistance. There were a lot of years between all of us and plenty of communication issues. However, I was surprised that it was me who got requested when challenges and personal difficulties occurred. That was an astounding triumph for our relationship.

To my siblings, I am enthused to know that you all lookup to me. That nugget made me realize that even though we didn't grow up together, I am the big sister and I care about my younger sisters and brothers. I want you all to know that I love you, and I want to see you overcome the obstacles that life presents. I want to give you an extra push to help you through the struggles that come with growing up. Here is a short list of four important lessons to live by that I have compiled. These are not all the lessons you will ever need in life. They are just a few that I believe can help you be a better you.

Life Lesson #1: Value

What do you value most? Is it yourself, the sneakers on your feet, the clothes on your back or your family? For some, it is hard to understand the concept of value. I'm not going to offer a textbook definition of value. Just think of value as being someone or something that you care about most. What do you hold near and dear to your heart? Your values encompass who you are. Your values tie into what makes you happy.

I challenge you to make a list of all the things and people that you care about most. Once that list is made, make it a point to implement those values daily. The number one value on that list should be YOURSELF. Valuing yourself helps you feel good about yourself and other people. Most important, your self-value influences the choices you make in life. Think about all the ways that you can respect yourself and those around you.

Life Lesson #2: Self-Acceptance

Now that you know what you value, you just made getting to know yourself a lot easier. Look at yourself in the mirror and ask yourself, "Who am I really?" You not only have an inner you, but also an outer you. What do you look like? Who do you look like? I am a firm believer in not separating my heritage or culture from who I am. Be proud of your heritage! Accept yourself just as you are and I promise that people around you will accept and love you for you. Don't be afraid to talk to your parents, grandparents and great-grandparents. Ask them questions about your family's history. Knowing where you come from will help you get to where you want to go in life. There are so many forces out here that want you to change who the Creator made you to be. Don't fall into the trap of believing that if you changed that one thing about yourself that you would be a better you. No, you would be a fake, a phony version of the real you. Every hair on your head is where it should be. You have unique gifts and talents to share with the world.

Life Lesson #3: Character Development

Think about all the things that make up your character. Is your character made up of good or bad traits? Do you know that your character has a huge impact on how people perceive you? Your character determines your destiny. Character entails how you think, your emotions, and how you act. Good character involves having morals or rules you live by, such as being kind, truthful, law abiding, and courageous. Can you identify people who are on the opposite side of the fence, such as people who lie, steal, cheat, and treat others unkindly? What side of the fence will you be on? I believe that an environment plays a big role in shaping our character. You don't have to be a product of your environment. Just because you grew up in a house full of thieves or drug dealers does not mean that this is your destiny. Just because a parent or a teacher spoke negatively of you does not mean you have to turn it into reality. Don't fall into the trap of believing them. You have choices, but it is up to you to make the right one.

Life Lesson #4: Opportunity

Have you ever sat in class and asked yourself, "Why am I learning this? What does this have to do with me?" Trust me, I've been there. Growing up, I've learned that education is one of the most important components of life. Without it, you become a prisoner of ignorance. School was not created to torture you. It helps you compete in society for opportunities, and it helps cultivate knowledge. Just like you have to nourish your body with food, you must nourish your mind with learning new ideas and concepts.

Although college can open more doors for you, education is not just about going to college. It is only a piece of the puzzle. Strive to be a life-long learner. Outside of school, read books and articles about everything that interests you. Soak it all in like a sponge. You will not believe all of the things that you can learn. I encourage you to discover things not included in your textbook. Take opportunities to volunteer and work in your community.

Learn how to make money the legal way. Feed your entrepreneurial spirit. Talk to adults who've been where you are or where you want to go. Don't be afraid to ask questions. There are no stupid questions. If you want to accomplish your dreams, you must value education and all that it has to offer. Opportunity does not greet you and knock on your door. You must seek it and go after it.

Jor'Danna

Admit

9

Set Myself Free

- Imprisoned For 22 Years, Sharon Payne *142*
- Don't Look Back, Jor'Danna Davis *145*
- Released, Now What?, Kenya Renee *147*
- Makes Me Normal, Human, Todd Parker *148*
- I Set Myself Free, Pamela S.B. Fagen *150*

Free Admission

IMPRISONED FOR 22 YEARS

This subject is very close to my heart. You see, I have a cousin on death row in Tennessee. He has been in a maximum-security prison since June 27, 1991, 22 years ago. I could sit here and write about how much we miss him or what's going on in the world since he's been locked up, but that would be kind of fruitless because he already knows. In fact, he probably knows more than we do because he has a TV in his 4 x 6 feet cell. He would be impressed though by the flat screen TVs, the iphones, and the digital cameras and how fast they work or the tablets and Kindles that are available. He would love the efficiency of cars. I'm positive that he's kept up with the latest fashions and shoe trends as well as hairstyles because each time I visit, he's always on par.

When he calls, we discuss things like the Iraq war, 911, diplomatic officials, and the latest invasion in the Ukraine. I'm sure he knows, through letters and pictures, the newest additions to the family as well as the passing of others. But, I'm sure that what he misses the most is his freedom—something we take for granted each day. You see, my cousin is innocent, and his innocence makes his imprisonment hard for my family. Because the supreme court's ruling was not to test the DNA that could so easily free him, and not to mention the disappearance of evidence, we are at a crossroads.

I wish I could say that he even cares about the everyday aspects of what we endure to stay in the game. Our routines of juggling marriages, kids, a job, and school, but that is not his concern. April 2007, December 2007, and January 2010 are milestones for him—days he was scheduled to die by execution or lethal injection. I can't imagine the strain of living that way and knowing you are innocent but having no one believe you.

So what has he missed? He was absent for his son's birthdays, first step, first tooth, first ride on a bike and his first days of school each year. All are milestones a parent cares about, and he worries about not being there for his son. The way it seems he won't see him at his high school and college graduations, getting married, or see his future grandchildren. Yes, that's what he'll miss, and we miss him.

Sharon Payne

"As I walked out the door toward the gate that would lead to my freedom, I knew if I didn't leave my bitterness and hatred behind, I'd still be in prison."

— Nelson Mandela

DON'T LOOK BACK

My secret shame is looking back in excess. I recall the Bible story of Lot and his family. God provided an entire city a chance to escape from Sodom and Gomorrah. They were offered the opportunity to avoid destruction, under the condition that they never took a look back. One verse from this Bible story really struck a chord, **"But his wife looked back behind him and she became a pillar of salt."** Almost like a movie, I play Genesis 19:26 in my head over and again. It is my wake-up call. As a result of giving in to reoccurring mind chatter of rebellious resentment, I realized that I became a "pillar of salt" one too many times. Each time that I let the shoulda-coulda-wouldas consume my mind, I am taken to a dark place in which there is no bright side. I get stuck in the past like a mouse in a glue trap. It is not my intent to suffer destruction from the fact that my father was not there for me. I can't let it get me down, even though it was due to his being addicted to street life and incarceration or enduring a childhood plagued with domestic violence and single-parent-family problems.

Throughout the years, this was the blame for overt self-criticism, depression, and aggression. When I noticed that this was a vicious cycle that could keep me in the dark as long as I let it, I started to force myself to forget about that chapter in my life. Ha! Who was I fooling? The past was still there, and it was haunting me. Each time someone let me down or something did not work out the way I wanted it to, I slid deeper down that slippery slope of despair. As I prayed and prayed for it to go away, the Creator revealed to me that it was never going away. I needed to accept that I could not outrun my past but use it as a catalyst for change. The first question that popped into my head was "How do I begin to do this?"

I'm an avid believer of knowing where you come from in order to know where you are going. There is something about that statement that keeps me humble. I was not going to let the past eat me alive. If anything, I was going to devour it and spit it out into something positive. Many believe that we are products of our environment. Statistically, I was supposed to be a teenage mother, a possible drug abuser, or an alcoholic who may have gotten incarcerated. I made a promise to myself that I was going to change the course of my life. Each time I wisely chose the company I kept or earned a degree, the past was placed behind me, serving as a reminder that I can triumph over it. As cliché as it sounds, I took those lemons and made them into lemonade!

I also discovered that forgiveness was another catalyst for change and a way to move forward. Realizing that was not an easy task for me because I had so much pinned-up animosity. For years, I kept score of who did this and that to me or who made me feel this and that way. I'm not saying that what they did was right. There's just no way possible for me to stay sane and be in good health by keeping tally marks on folks. No one is perfect! For a long time, I was so angry at my father for not being the man that I wanted him to be. I'd blame him for everything that went wrong and every wrong feeling that I felt. For example, whenever I got into a minor disagreement with my husband, it resulted into something bigger, with me screaming at the top of my lungs, breaking something, and being pissed for the rest of the day. I knew that I was wrong. I justified my actions by saying,
"Well, I get my temper from him" (my father) or "It's because you did something that reminded me of him." As soon as I accepted my father for who he is and stopped blaming him, I was able to take responsibility for my own anger issues.

Through lots of self-reflection, I learned that accepting myself was a big key to not letting the past hold me hostage. Even though I had some experiences that were meant to break me or turn me into a statistic, I could not let those experiences make me love myself any less. Accepting the journey that the Creator allowed me to travel gives me peace. Yes, it has shaped every piece of my being. Sometimes it might seem like I have an attitude or I appear to be too reserved or too quiet for your liking. I am an intelligent thinker who won't sweat the small stuff. I am sensitive but strong-willed. I will not apologize for being who I am! Take me as I am! There is no looking back because I've been set free! Everyone has baggage left over from their journey. It's what you do with it that makes the difference. I had the option to let the baggage weigh me down and depress me or lift me up to make me stronger.

Jor'Danna

RELEASED, NOW WHAT?

(A letter to those released from prison)

Sistergirl and brother man walk a straight path. Freedom, as you know it, is conditional, so enjoy it while it lasts. Look beyond the clouds my friend and you will see the one who's truly in your corner. There will be many distractions but also signs and warnings to help you on your path.

When people start to judge you, don't point the finger. There will be those soul stealers and drug dealers trying to take you back down that wide road to destruction. But look up to the sky my friend because He is the healer.

Justify your purpose because when you don't have one, you walk aimlessly through the wilderness of life. Realize it's your life you must enrich. I'm writing from the heart. This is not a sales pitch.

You are smarter than others think. Your intelligence is echoed by everyone you meet, so walk in your individualism. Show them you are diligent. My friend, I am not your enemy! Do not harm me because I will not harm you. You can beat the odds. Remember that redemption is the key. "A dream is reality in the making."

Sincerely,

Kenya Renee

Free Admission

MAKES ME NORMAL, HUMAN

She never had her emotions in check.
And I knew that.
I took advantage of the admission
for her submission.
It was plentiful, and I knew better.
I tread lightly, like a feather,
through her defenses.
Atomic dogmatic. Flesh heathen breathing.
Gimme, I said!
The guy I turned into makes it look like my mom shouldn't be praised.
Before my inner reply, say goodbye, to time.
Time upon timeliness.
A photo reminds me of some good times, a tad.
But there were equal amounts of bad.
What put the doo in this hickey was unforgivable.
He was inconceivable.
Unbelievable, by me.
We all face challenges as they come, go, and stay. Someone has to.
Allow me to plead with you.
Let us be, as close to normal as possible.
How could you?
He is not from me.

Access to the Soul

Time upon timeliness.
How do I loathe thee?
You say acknowledgment is what it's all about.
Yet, I have my insurmountable doubts.
Is there any normalcy within our mockery of adulthood.
If I could, I'd forget our encounter, many summers upon timeliness ago.
I'd neglected the smearing of names like a jam, the back, forth and so and so.
I grew as it grew. Forgiveness for whom?
You know what, the hell with it all, you win, except for the grand prize.
The respect levels fluctuated like a dieter's size.
My guilt was soon minimized.
I wish I could manifest myself in the past, and not at random.
Take more time with listening to her ask me, "Did you wear a condom?"
Maybe this time science pays me a visit in the form of an embryo.
Wouldn't my parents be proud though?
What a way to settle down, settle in and settle for the normal life.
Many a man have been hit with this particular stack of bricks.
Some men choose to father up until it fits.
Others figure, they can at least be father figures.
My ban on society's ideal man becomes bigger.
Deal with it. And while you, world, are dealing with that,
I'll just continue to keep my own form of normalcy intact.
I've been groomed for future trying times due to some past crying times.
But I live me, free.
Pay my emotional dues even if it means I lose.

Todd Parker

I SET MYSELF FREE

I SET MYSELF FREE.
I AM FREE, ANYWAY,
I'M INSPIRED TO BE.

Free to be me!
a lover,
a mother,
a friend,
a success,
a woman,
and anything I need to be.
I was designed to be free.

I SET MYSELF FREE.
I AM FREE, ANYWAY,
I'M INSPIRED TO BE.

What am I to be ashamed of?
Why should I be ashamed?
Ignorance was never made to hinder me.
I am free to be me:
to express,
to create,
to give,
to receive,
to act or not act,
to create my own style.

**I SET MYSELF FREE.
I AM FREE, ANYWAY,
I'M INSPIRED TO BE.**

My past is behind me.
It teaches me and it keeps me humble.
I don't fear my past, it's already done.
I don't have to run from it.
There is nothing in the past that I'm afraid of,
want to cover, or am hiding from.
I welcome it.
Therefore, come.
Let the past come out,
Let it reveal the messages that were missed.
Let the past teach us all.
Let's discern what not to do today.
Let's forgive each other.
Let's find a way to move forward.

**I SET MYSELF FREE.
YOU KNOW I AM FREE.
BECAUSE OF MY CREATIVITY.**

I can recreate.
I can resurrect as needed
the outer expressions of my life.
The external appearances can always change
to reflect the rewrites of my inner self,

Free Admission

the renewal of my interior,
and my overall spiritual rebirth.
Natural and spiritual freedom has been issued
and favorably received throughout the
universe.
We just need to receive it. Let it come.

I SET MYSELF FREE.
I AM FREE. ANYWAY,
GOD SAYS THIS IS ME
AND ONLY HE CAN SET ME FREE

Pamela S.B. Fagen

Admit 10

Cost of Celebrity

- The Price, J.D. Cooper & Pamela S. B. Fagen *155*
- The Cost To Be The Boss, Kenya Renee *157*
- A Minute Of Fame, Jor'Danna Davis *158*

THE PRICE

Recently, I interviewed an accomplished actress who prefers to remain anonymous. I asked her about her thoughts on being a celebrity. She expressed to me that being recognized and celebrated publicly for her accomplishments in her craft, at one time, was gratifying. Then she looked at me frowning and said, "That is what you want, but what you get is not worth the price you have to pay. It costs you, living every day in the public eye. Your name gets smeared through the rumor mill and everything you do is distorted in gossip columns. The most horrifying things for me are the infatuation of stalkers and the exploitation that goes on in the industry."

She went on to tell me that she found out the hard way that you must pay a huge price to become famous. She admitted that the familiarity is nice but it is negated by people taking advantage of you. She continued with a sad countenance.

"You are no longer your own person, and that is a hard pill to swallow. You have to adhere to the public's unquenchable thirst to know every detail about you. Privacy comes at a premium price that no celebrity can afford—after all, you need an audience, and you can't do without your fans."

She told me that once a man called to book her for an audition the following day. She thought nothing of it. She jotted down the address and drove to the location at the scheduled time. Once there, she didn't notice any signs of an event being held as she entered the dark building. The next thing she knew, someone grabbed her from behind and put a cloth over her nose and mouth. She said she immediately lost consciousness. When she woke up, she found herself face down on a bed, being violated by three men. She said she begged God to let her die. Apparently, she did not die, but she attempted to step out of the limelight for a while since no one did anything about the assaults she endured.

She explained that, to her horror and disbelief, the incident brought her worldwide attention when the film was released. After the movie aired, she went back to the authorities and questioned how they could get away with recording such a horrendous crime. During the investigation, the producers said they had proof that it was all a mutually agreed upon rehearsed movie production. Again, no one believed her when she insisted otherwise. She said, it took a while, but with counseling and prayer, she was able to recover from the attack and the unplanned accolades she received from her industry.

"What did you learn from that experience?" I asked.

She looked me eyeball to eyeball and said, "I'm blessed to have gotten out of that situation alive, but it got me more work. For most celebrities, with fame comes a price—and that cost is the loss of your privacy, dignity, and sometimes your soul."

"Do you believe it is worth the price?"

Instantly her posture straightened, her eyes lit up, and she smiled with a charismatic look on her face as if in front of a camera.

"The rewards are the techno-color lifestyle you get to live, the **diamond-studded** status you receive, your performances on the **silver** screen, earning plenty of **green**. You are a **golden** hot commodity on the market and you can take that walk down the **red** carpet. Even when you fade to **black** in death you are immortalized forever."

That question certainly received an interesting response. It was the first time during our interview that her mood was upbeat, and she delivered her answer with pride and dynamic passion.

My last question was, "What advice would you pass on to those seeking notoriety?"

"Mmmm," she moaned. Her eyes glazed over and she sank back into her former melancholy mood.

"This industry is cut throat and only the strong survive. So, be careful what you wish for—because you just might get it, and some of it you don't want."

I thanked her for the interview and for being candid and courageous enough to bring exposure to her ordeal.

J.D. Cooper and Pamela S. B. Fagen

Access to the Soul

THE COST TO BE THE BOSS

Your soul has sold out, all for clout in society.
The notoriety has caused those once grounded,
the most well-rounded, to lose their mind.
All corrupted by a small but powerful group of like kinds.
At the same time, increased their bank accounts
in unthinkable large amounts.
But the more money, the more problems.
Funny, they still have troubles, and money can't solve 'em.
Limitless one-hundred dollar bills to count.
Now it's The Most High you denounce—what's that about.
Go head little duffle bag boy.
The price of fame, is contingent upon
how many lives you destroy with your lyrics.
Pondering on what type of final price you will pay.
Addicted to that thing called FAME.
Now everyone knows your name.
Millions follow you.
Now you're a role model, yet you say you're not to blame.
Such a shame, how you use the Lord's name in vain.
What's the price? What did you sacrifice?
Please don't tell me it was a loved one's life!
Quick to yell things aren't always what they seem.
You gleam on the big screen.
On the "A" list.
In private only a select few know you're really a fiend.
You looked really nice on the cover of that magazine.
You are in love with the GREEN.
So, in the end it's GOD and you, no one in between.
But who am I to judge because I too have dreams.
And I believe that if you ask you shall receive
and He will provide all your needs if you have the faith of a mustard seed.
If it's His WILL, it can happen, but stay equipped with the entire amour because the
price of fame may just take you under.

Kenya Renee

A MINUTE OF FAME

Give her a minute of fame, just one, so she can feel good about herself and be a household name.

She'll do anything to have it, even if it makes her feel some shame.

She doesn't have to be an actress in a box office movie, she's got YouTube and Instagram.

She got her minute of fame.

Let her think of the most ignorant thing to say so she can get paid.

Let her be that girl that you get to know on her own reality show.

Jumping off tables, throwing bottles, wretchedness is her motto, as long as she gets her minute of fame.

He kills an innocent person and plays the victim as though the person is to blame.

With the help of the media, the private and intimate moments are all on video for the world to see. Stuck in cyberspace for all eternity.

Using your body to get to the top. Know that this life cannot be lived nonstop.

Remember, you only get a minute of fame.

When family and friends disappear and your money is your sidekick. When you come down from your high, do you still want that minute of fame?

Being a celebrity is like an addiction.

You're living a life of contradictions. It is easier to attain than thought. For the price of the soul, it is bought.

Jor'Danna

Admit

11

Facing Bullies

- The Courage To Fight, Sharon Payne *160*
- Bound By A Bully, Jor'Danna *162*
- Spotlight On Bullying, Sharon Payne *165*
- Wolf Ticket, Pamela S.B. Fagen *166*
- WAR, Kenya Renee *169*

Free Admission

THE COURAGE TO FIGHT

One beautiful, sunny summer day in the 1970s, my younger brother came home yelling and crying that an older boy who was a bully in our neighborhood had knocked him off his bike.

I was the oldest and I didn't let anyone pick on my siblings. I was a girl, but I was tough. I asked him to show me how it happened. My brother started to act out the whole scene. He said, "I rode around the block and as I rounded the corner by our house, the older boy who lives diagonally across from us walked in the middle of the street and pushed me clean off the bike." My brother had skinned his knees and elbow. I asked my brother with a look of concern, "Are you alright?" He said, "Yes!" I told him, "We will settle this today." I grabbed his hand and we both walked over to the bully and asked him to come here. He was leaning against the house on his porch sizing us up. Now mind you, I wore a sundress, flip flops and a pony tail while this guy had on jeans, gym shoes, and a T-shirt.

I look him square in the eye and I said, to him, "Did you knock my brother off the bike?"

"Yeah" he says, "And I'll do it again!"

I said, "Oh Really?"

I look down at my brother who was standing next to me and I said to him,

"You get back on that bike, ride around the block at top speed, and I want to see if he's gonna knock you off that bike again while I'm standing here!"

So, off my brother went at full speed pedaling on that bike like his life depended on it! Sure enough, when he got close to the guy, the bully took his whole hand and pushed my brother clean off the bike! Ooooh, I was so mad! All I could see was red! Before I knew what had happened, I pounced on him like a lion. I tore into him so fast, he didn't even know what hit him. I knocked him down, sat on top of him and swung blow after blow until he started hollering for help and his nose bled!

His mom, who was also my mom's friend, came out and tried to get me off of him, but I was too persistent to teach this guy a lesson. His mom started pulling my sundress which began to choke me. Before I knew it, I called her a bitch and said, "Let me go!" I looked at her face and saw the hurt in her eyes. I stopped hitting him and saw my mom coming across the street. My mom was 5'3", but she could bring you down to size with her words. Plus, she was old-school and always believed an adult over children when it came to verifying information. So, as soon as the lady started telling my mom what I said, she yelled at me to go in the house. Boy was I angry! Didn't anybody care to hear my side of the story?

My 6'7" 250 lb. dad met me in the driveway as I stomped back into the house and asked what happened. He could see that I was pretty upset. I took a deep breath and explained the whole incident to him. He looked at me for a while and told me to go sit on the front porch. Then, he walked across the street. I saw him point to the house. He apparently told my brother and mom to go home too. I couldn't hear anything, but I could see my dad nodding his head. All I could think about was how I was going to get a spanking for this one. My mom and little brother marched across the street and looked at me as they passed by the porch. My mom had a furious look on her face and she fussed, seemingly to herself, and I knew she was mad as all get out. My brother smiled at me as he followed our mom.

After waiting for what seemed like an eternity, I saw my dad walk back across the street. He asked, "Are you alright?" I looked at him and said, "Yes Sir!" I will never forget the smile and the look of pride he gave me when he said, "Good job" and walked away. I smiled and sat there just looking at the sky. Life was so good. I had taught the neighborhood bully a lesson that day!

The only regret I have is that I never went to apologize to Ms. Beverly for calling her out of her name before she passed. She was a loyal friend to my mother and a great educator in our community. I'll love her forever.

Sharon Payne

BOUND BY A BULLY

As Shelly stared at herself in the oval, silver-rimmed bedroom mirror, she traced the dark circles around her eyes.

"I have to do something about this," she said in disgust.

"I'm letting myself go, big time."

Her husband Steve's voice echoed in her mind, "You need to lose some weight and get rid of that weave." Shelly sunk into her purple chaise lounge chair, wrapped herself up into a thick blanket and closed her eyes. She imagined being in another place in another time. She was sick of being picked on by the very man who was supposed to protect and love her unconditionally until death does them part. It wasn't like Steve was that much of a looker. He was short, stubby, and bald. He was a man with a Napoleon complex. Shelly actually did him a favor by dating him in the first place. When they met eight years prior, Shelly was fit and curvy, with a smile that could melt any man's heart.

It seemed like it was just yesterday that they met. It was in the middle of the summer and Shelly was hanging out with her best friend, Kayla, at a neighborhood music festival. Steve approached her at one of the food vendor booths. His eyes remained on her chest while he talked about how nice the festival was and how good she looked. She was intrigued by his confidence but not instantly attracted to him. It took a few dates before she really had feelings for him. One year later, they had a destination wedding in Puerto Rico.

The sound of the front door slamming startled her. Anxiety flooded her body.

"You didn't clean up?"

Steve yelled up the stairs. The sound of his footsteps coming up the stairs made her anxiety worse. Shelly pretended that she was sleeping so that he wouldn't bother her.

Steve peeked his head into the room and saw that she was resting. He grabbed the floral blanket from off her large-frame body and chastised her for not cleaning the house and lying in bed all day.

It was her day off from a tiring six-day workweek as an interior designer. Why couldn't he let her rest? She didn't understand.

It was not as if Steve had a demanding job. His job as a so-called virtual assistant entailed sitting in front of the computer in their home office for hours on end. He used to be a virtual assistant at a prestigious law firm. Steve quit because he was tired of answering to authority. It was clear that Shelly was the breadwinner. If it weren't for her, he would have nothing.

Shelly slowly got up and walked down to the kitchen to begin washing the dishes. Memories of her past warped her mind. She envisioned her father complaining that she wasn't smart enough and that she wasn't a go-getter like her older sister with whom she shared a different mother. Shelly did not have a close relationship with her sister, Taryn. Taryn was ten years older than Shelly, and she lived overseas because of her husband's military career.

Shelly's mother died when she was only eight years old. She had little memory of her mother. The only thing she remembered was her embrace. She always had the tightest hugs. After her mother had passed away, her father took care of her and her sister. He now lived in a retirement home that was 2 hours away. Shelly rarely visited because she didn't want to hear his put-downs about why she wasn't this or wasn't that. She never thought in a million years that she would end up married to someone that seemed to be a carbon copy of her father.

Shelly came to the conclusion that she was bullied her whole life. She never had many friends and often was excluded from cliques because of her weight.

"I'm tired of this shit!" Shelly whispered. She tossed the wet dishes across the room in a fit of rage. Glass shattered on the bright yellow walls and white ceramic floor. Shelly crouched down in the corner and sobbed loudly. Steve ran down the stairs into the kitchen.

"What the hell is going on, I'm trying to work! I thought I told you to clean up, not destroy my damn house!"

Shelly screamed, "Your house, this is my house!"

She jumped up and grabbed a large glass and threw it at him. Dodging the glass, he slipped, fell and hit the side of his head on the edge of the granite counter top. Steve whimpered and held the side of his head. Shelly saw that blood began to drip down the side of his face. She ran upstairs, grabbed a duffel bag, and stuffed it with as many of her belongings as she could. She ran downstairs with the bag and swiped the car keys to her Range Rover off of the counter top. She looked down and saw that Steve seemed unconscious and was still bleeding. She walked quickly out the front door into the driveway and sped off.

She didn't know where she was going, she just needed to go. She didn't know whether Steve was still breathing, and at that point, she really didn't care. There was no better time to break free. After 3 hours of driving, She stopped to grab dinner at a fast food restaurant. As she sunk her teeth into her sandwich, reality sunk into her mind. She banged her fist on the steering wheel and screamed, **"What did I do, what did I do?!"**

As much as she hated Steve, she certainly didn't want him to die. After calming down, she drove to a hotel. She knew her mind was not in the right place. Maybe she could make more sense of this in the morning. Maybe this was a bad dream that she would awake from soon. At around 3 A.M, the sound of her cell phone ringing startled her awake. She looked down at the screen and saw Steve's name. Shelly froze in fear.

Jor'Danna

SPOTLIGHT ON BULLYING

It didn't happen overnight. It was a progression of pressure and aggravation that simmered underneath an abusive hand of neglect and an urge that threatened to consume more than it was fed.

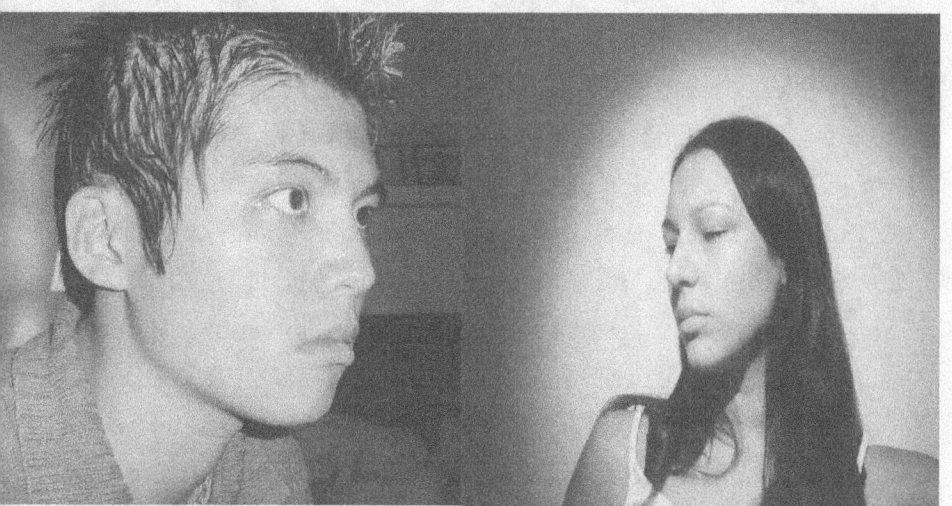

The thrill of dominating someone without permission turns them on. Only a BULLY knows the Pleasure of Pain and ignores the Price of Pressure. If the BULLIES don't stop and learn to love instead of hate, they will become prey, devoured by a brutal and detrimental fate.

Sharon Payne

WOLF TICKET

It is midwinter, and the season is already brutal and hard to bare. The holiday season is over. Most people are in debt and existing on a thin line of patience from the commercial industry selling its wolf ticket. We are prompted to spend, spend, and spend to make our lives merrier.

Positive memories and hopes for a prosperous spring and summer season fuel my optimism. It doesn't last long. I'm now feeling the pressure of many obligations that are costing me time and causing me emotional distress.

The political campaigning season has arrived again. Every politician sells us a wolf ticket, promising hope. I receive flyers in my door way and messages on voice mail. They're all geared toward telling me to vote for this cause or that cause. To vote this party or that party. Please come to this meeting at this church, center, or hotel. This is average day-to-day life in the big city.

Somewhere in the shadows is a ticket. The ticket reads free admission, issued by the bully. Is it a wolf ticket?

The festivals, carnivals, and circuses are coming to town. Already you can smell the aroma of street foods luring people from everywhere. There will be plenty of grilled, chilled, smothered, and pickled foods flooding the menu and prepared to keep your taste buds asking for more. All the local churches and businesses are supporting the events. Everyone will get a free wolf ticket, and the blessings are also free. Be there or be square. The tickets are usually priced at $20 each. To get your free ticket, you must arrive between 9 and 11 A.M. You can't leave before 4 P.M. The usual price will be charged to those arriving or leaving at other times, no exceptions. You must purchase at least one chicken dinner at $10 for adults and $8 for children 12 years and under. Outside food and beverages are not allowed. We have a special treat for you this year. All rides will be at one low price of $3 per ride. Booklets with 12 tickets each for $30 will be available also. Many other amenities will be available at special rates. Fifty percent of all proceeds will go back to the church of your choice.

A special chance to win big is available this year for those who stay until the end. A large wheel of fortune will be waiting for you at the exit. For $20, those that stay until the end will have a chance to spin the big wheel. The fortune is $20,000. If you are the winner, you go home with $10,000 free and clear with all taxes paid. The remainder of the prize will go to your church or selected charity. Don't be a drag, stay until the end for a chance to spin. Win and be a blessing to others.

GET YOUR FREE TICKETS!
GET YOUR FREE BLESSINGS!

The bully can be characterized as someone or some entity that wants to use its power or personal force for personal or collective gain. It has the tendency to use fear, reward, pain, loss, bondage, confusion, etc. to push its agenda. A major motivator for the bully is the control of people, situations, or money. You may often hear the bully say, "If it isn't my way, it's the highway," "If it's not my way, it's no way," "If you don't do what I want or give me what I want, I will hurt you," or worst of all, "If I can't have it and have it my way, then I'll kill for it." Ouch!

FREE TICKETS TO THE MUSEUM,
FEATURING THE "FAMILIAR" BULLIES

Childhood bullies are the boys and girls who terrorize other boys and girls because they don't like what they represent, are different from them, or have something that they want. The differences may be that they are skinny, fat, acne prone, nerdy, wealthy, on a different sports team, of a different race, etc. The intent of the bullies is to take without asking or ridicule the victims to the point of destroying their self-esteem, reputation, confidence, and relationships. Bullies usually resort to violence, such as fighting and damaging property, to express themselves. Sometimes the bullies are in pain themselves and the only way they know how to relieve the pain is to hurt someone else. It's a well-known fact that "hurting people, hurt people."

Children can be the cruelest of all bullies. The damage can be great and irreversible. Many childhood bullies become adult bullies if their behavior is allowed to persist.

The classic bully type is the rapist that attacks women, children, and men for the purpose of sexual satisfaction, degrading the victim, or establishing perceived power. The classic bully sometimes appears as a racist or sexist person who only sees the world by race or sex and claims to be superior in his/her view. The bully can be the pimp who exploits women and children by selling sex for profit. The bully can be a slave holder that buys and sell people and ideas for personal and financial gain. The bully can be someone who beats his/her spouse to establish some false sense of control. The nontraditional bully is the organization that exploits victims of disease by using them in unethical research, many times without their knowledge or gain, and sells a wolf ticket disguised as hope for a cure that belies their intent to further science.

DID YOU RECOGNIZE ANY OF THOSE BULLIES?

Understand that the bully uses any means necessary to achieve his or her objectives. The most common tools used by the bully are fear, pain, loss, slander, isolation, and blackmail. All bullies operate using the same old tactics. The common denominator is someone or entity that uses knowledge, power, pain, expertise, etc. to take advantage of others. However, the Bible says, "There is nothing new under the sun." The same tricks that got Eve are the same devices bullies are using today.

Finally, I must say that the face of the bully is real. The face of the bully wears many masks. The face of the bully is found in all venues.

Pamela S. B. Fagen

WAR

Another war has begun.
How many lives must be lost before this one is won?
Missiles are what they hear.
Silence, the whistle, and the boom.
Our soldiers think their time has come.
Eighteen and nineteen year old's die too soon,
looking east, directly at the moon.
The main question: what are we fighting for?
I've lost count. Does anyone know anymore.
Some say its power. The majority gossips of oil.
They're attacking us on U.S. soil.
Right now who cares?
Let us support our soldiers because they stand loyal.
They are dying for us,
something gangbangers would never be courageous enough to do.
First there was Bush II, Sadaam and his crew,
and now a new group called ISIS too.
Troops are dying, being killed by friendly fire attacks.
Many of our troops are seized and aren't coming back.
POWs are of all races, have a variety of colored faces.
Our men and women fight in foreign places,
but come home still hated by the racists.
U.S. citizens display signs of protest.
We must have our soldiers' interests at best—unlimited premium
health care at best and zero home loan interest.
It's our daily lives they protect.
Every day, I watch CBS, NBC, ABC and CNN
in the end hoping the United States will win.
It's not about the president's approval rate.
It's not about his re-election date.
It's about our soldiers living to see their next birthday. I pray.

Kenya Renee

Admit

12

Free Write

- Broken Glass, Jor'Danna Davis 172
- Pulse Of Today, Pamela S. B. Fagen 173
- Help Me Understand, Kenya Renee 176
- I Can't Stop Now, Sharon Payne 178
- Just Breathe, Todd Parker 180

Free Admission

BROKEN GLASS

Sparkling reflections of the ghetto
Shabby homes, wild, sad, and vicious creatures
The corner is home to many men
Children look for love and cry on the bosoms of the old
Their streets crowded with sin
Broken glass leading to a path of a lost soul
Sharpness offends hearts of gold
Daydreams of a better place fill the tainted air
Victims of oppression shattered into **broken glass**,
not intended to last.

Jor'Danna

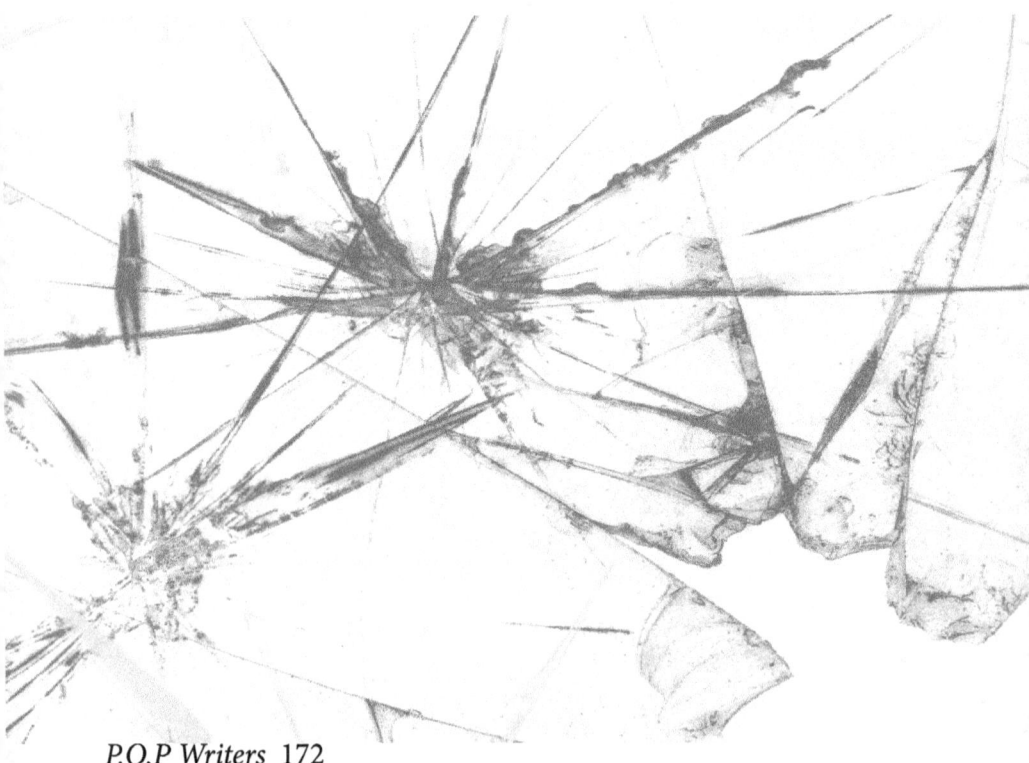

PULSE OF TODAY

Dear Today, the Present, and Right Now,

I have the task of addressing you in this year of 2014. In the month of May, the weather this year has been very unseasoned. That is somewhat typical of the times we live in today. Seasons have always represented a certain attitude and a spirit, which we anticipate and enter into with certain expectations. It doesn't cost us anything to enter into a season. The seasons allow free admission. However, our expectations may cost us dearly, and that's the ticket we hold. We expect a season of winter to last three months, but it costs us six months. We expect 10 to 15 inches of snow, but we paid the price for 40 inches or more. So it is, with today's seasonal blend of things. We expect certain things to happen because it's typical of the season and/or the times we live in. However, the happenings of today, the present, and right now are less than we expect in many situations.

"If you want to make enemies, try to change something."

—**Woodrow Wilson**

This is a time of judgment. Many judge and jury programs and attitudes exist in our world of media today, the present, and right now. Admission to these programs and attitudes is usually free.

This is a season of freedom and peace. We live in a land that supports civil rights and liberties by law. We are not fighting a major civil war at this time. Based on that understanding, our expectations are to feel free and secure in every way.

Many of us are grossly disappointed by the season. Our expectations are met with contrasting, or unseasoned, attitudes. Minor things such as traveling within the states and even mingling with different faiths are viewed negatively. I've been criticized for visiting family and friends in other states. They call it looking back or hind-sightedness. This is absurd and a negative attitude in this season, as most people visit friends and family where ever they are and as many times as they can. In some cases, law abiding citizens are punished for doing the expected—that is traveling, mingling, voting, corresponding (written and telephones), looking for work, dating, etc. Many of us are not sure why we are treated like criminals in our own land. We are exercising our right to live and move around freely, as we should. Our phones are monitored and some calls are blocked or intercepted, our mail is read or monitored, our travel is watched and followed, etc. This is highly irregular during a season of freedom and peace.

"The dogmas of the quiet past are inadequate to the stormy present. The occasion is piled high with difficulty, and we must rise—with the occasion. As our case is new, so we must think anew, and act anew. We must disenthrall ourselves, and then we shall save our country."

—Abraham Lincoln

This is a season and time of technology, innovation, and progression. We live in a land where everyone is looking for the next big thing. We search for that thriving business, that new medical breakthrough, and that recipe for success. We marvel and boast about the concept of free enterprise. Come to America, come and hang your shingle out, start your business, and be innovative and free. However, many of those expectations are crushed when we are faced with backward practices of racial and sexual discrimination. We thought that such practices had been eradicated. However, it appears to be a new business.

Primitive abuse of women for breeding purposes still exists today and is blatantly discussed. Many of the abusers are desperate and do not respect age, sex, or race. The cause of such desperation is unknown to me. We recently heard about the kidnapping of more than 200 school girls in Africa. The abuse is highly imaginable in terms of what has happened to these girls. It's a wake-up call to all nations that human trafficking and the forced breeding of children exist. The children may never know both parents.

Can you imagine men being forced to ejaculate to produce sperm? Also to be envisioned are girls and women lying sedated and inseminated against their will. They often have no memory of the event. The silencing of individuals will not silence the abuse. The vaginas will scream out, and the penises will create a riot. How do you think people are made aware of these things? Truly, the very rocks that we stand on will cry out. In a season of high technology, innovation, and progress, you would think societies would know of another way to have children other than forcing someone to breed. Maybe the old-fashioned way is better. That is, meet a nice woman/man, get married willingly, and have children, if you both agree.

"Most of our assumptions have outlived their uselessness."

—Marshall Mc Luhan

"He that will not apply new remedies must expect new evils; for time is the greatest innovator."

—Francis Bacon

What is today?
Today is that magic moment you spoke of yesterday and called it tomorrow.
"The greatest danger in times of turbulence is not the turbulence; it is to act with yesterday's logic."

—Peter Drucker

"Change is the law of life and those who look only to the past or present are certain to miss the future."

—John F. Kennedy

"Every generation needs a new revolution."

—Thomas Jefferson

I've shared a lot with you. I solicited help from the past through the quotations that compliment this letter. These are just a few pulsations of today, the present, and right now. Believe me, I could go on. My words are strong and deliberate, but there is no need to be fearful. Don't be afraid of me. Take your index finger and thumb and place them under your chin, in the hollow between the windpipe and the large muscle in the neck. Press lightly until you feel a pulse. Do you have the spot? Does it frighten you? Listen and feel your inner beat. That's me at the pulse, and we've got a lot of work to do. I'm not a leader for this season, just part of the pulse. Fear not. If it's any comfort to you, I will let you know when it's time to be afraid.

Pamela S. B. Fagen

HELP ME UNDERSTAND

I don't understand how you can say
that you would like a woman who is strong,
But it is her that you are constantly mistreating
and doing wrong.
In public, you're so appreciative.
But you don't cherish her, and that's abusive.

It's acceptable in your eyes to take money
out of the home to take multiple women on dates.
But at the end of the night,
you're looking in that hotel mirror with self-hate.
Maybe it's in your family's trait.

More seriously, why do you risk your life
and the lives of others for a piece of ass?
Doesn't your wife please you with her sass?
Isn't she sensual, romantic and have class?
I don't understand!

Julie M. Hollowa

Okay, your wife cooks and cleans—plate ready when you walk in the door.
You wake up one day talking about you're not in love with her anymore.
The one you said vows to, you no longer adore,
because you've been knock, knock, knocking on that whore's door.
Say goodbye to your blessings 'cause if she's anything like me,
her prayers will be answered.
Prosperity in your future—NO MORE!

She never cheated, worked when you could not,
and unequally paid all the bills.
When you were sick, it was you she healed. You never missed a meal.
She has always been a giver. From you she would never steal.

I don't understand
because she has always had your back.

Art by: Julie M. Holloway

Why is it respect that you lack?
Oh, I know. You lack respect for self. It's proven. That's a fact.

Please help me understand.
Please don't tell me it's because you are a man.
There is a difference between a man and a male.

To my understanding,
it's the head of our family lines that break down and fail.
Remember you're the head and not the tail.
No more blaming the weaker vessel.
The Woman—she's a good thing! What the Hell!

Kenya Renee

Free Admission

I CAN'T STOP NOW

Even though I know I'm doing wrong, right now I cannot stop.

You see, my image I have to keep up, and try to sell these rocks.

While my pockets are getting fatter, the hypes' eyes are getting madder.

I'll sell to your momma, daddy, sister, and brother;

while this rock screams to your organs, let's kill each other.

I've got my car, rims, spokes, and a grill.

Oh and the ladies, I can call on a whim.

You may think that we would never meet

when in fact, I could live right down the street.

See someday, I'd like to stop and enjoy life—

settle down, find me a wife,

take care of my kids, and go back to school.

But to stop right now, I'd be a fool.

I know I need to seek God's face,

But not now, business will go to waste.

You see, I'm on a mission just to please.

No hard work for me, a life of ease.

Until one day, I was standing around

waiting for customers making their rounds—

shooting the breeze, hanging with folks,

laughing and smoking, and telling some jokes.

Up pulled a guy, said he wanted a rock.

Went in his shirt and pulled out a glock.

I didn't even see it, no time to run.

The impact of the bullets felt like a ton.

Hey, I don't have time to die I screamed in my head

as my breath faded away and then I was dead.

You see my friend life isn't fair.

You reap what you sow, and you sow what you cared.

The moral of this story is never live fast.

Or you could pay the cost for your evil past.

So start life over and do well and have fun.

So the Master can say, "Servant well done."

Sharon Payne

Free Admission

JUST BREATHE

Once upon one night. Or any night. One is all it takes for that amazin' one.
That infamous she-thing that persuades you some.
You got that 'I don't feel like going out face.'
all over the place.
Libation in one hand while the other gives love,
when suddenly…
luvvy duvvy.
It ain't easy
cuz she's teasing
the painted thoughts you had when you dreamt you were a painter.
She was the subject.
So I pull the move that fine women choose to get looked at.
I make myself noticeable within a five-foot radius.
Her vicinity
breaks down that geometry,
and the scent-----must be Vicki. Secret? Yeah.
Next time she breezes by me,
I'll kiss, squeeze, hug and feel.
Damn, I touched her creamy center, and it's real.
One look with one touch on one night by one woman and she had my heart racing a

Access to the Soul

greyhound being chased by a cheetah.
Stone cold K-Swiss fan but she turned me into an Adidas man.
So all day I dream about sizing up her puma and the cat, the cat,
the catastrophic way that she...
The long island awaits my lips
but if the light vodka cancels the dark rum
then that leaves the gin that burns the throat,
collapses a lung
and I'm back at square one,
all over again.
And I'm not even her friend.
I held my breath as she left.
But Dollface, I'm intellectual and slick, ask Jeff.
I held back sexual
cuz I see someone next to you
co-signin' me looking at you.
The word could spread that I'm head of the committee on pleasing you.
Her mental reveals she's got learning to do,
to be available.
For a guy like me, true.
One of those nights, with that 'one of those nights' face.
At least until the mature lady vibrates...

Todd Parker

Free Admission

> **There is nothing to writing. All you do is sit down at a typewriter and bleed.**
>
> —Ernest Hemingway

PRESENTING THE
P.O.P Writer's

Kizzy Givens • Todd Parker • Kenya Renee • Jor'Danna Davis
Pamela S.B. Fagen • Katerria "Starr" Doty • Sharon Payne

Kizzy Mernice Givens

Kizzy Mernice Beasley-Givens was born to the proud parents Sandra Bernice Beasley and David Green Sr. on May 21, 1977. She was a child very loved and full of life. She had six brothers and five sisters. Kizzy has always spoken her mind from the first time she was able to form sentences, I believe. If she did not like something, she told you; if she did like something, she told you. You could not ask her opinion if you were not ready for what would come out of her mouth. In so many words, she would check you regardless of whether you felt you deserved it.

She was in many activities over the years at school. Kizzy's siblings used to call her the Rolling Reporter because she would tell everything she saw, but, if she thought you needed to be defended, she'd fight for you to the bitter end. She was the fairest person that I have known; she did not allow her emotions to cloud her judgment. She believed right is right and wrong is wrong.

Kizzy had long-lasting relationships with friends Katerria, Jackie, and Krystal. These young ladies were friends since high school and were there until the end of Kizzy's journey. She was also blessed to meet two women that she called her Cancer Sisters: Karen (Kirk) Roberts and Tammy (Michael) Miller. Kizzy embraced the old saying of a person who "never met a stranger." When her best friend Tonya entered her life, she brought the love of Kizzy's life, Anthony Givens. Kizzy felt that she was blessed to meet, fall in love with, and marry her soul mate, Anthony Givens. Their family consisted of their daughters—Parisha, Kassandra, and Nyssa—and the family dog, Rocko.

Kizzy had to overcome many obstacles in her life. She overcame losing her mother at a young age, she was abused, and endured the biggest battles of all when she received a cancer diagnosis not once but twice. She always kept her warrior spirit, but know she was the "Warrior that Won!"

Kizzy Givens was a founding member of the non-for-profit organization Envision Life. The Envision Life website is www.envisionlifecorp.org

Todd Parker

Todd has been writing since high school. He was first turned on to writing poetry and short stories by his English teacher. He kept up the hobby all through college and afterward. He even read poetry throughout the city of Chicago, where he was born and raised. He inspires the students he mentors, using the power of the written and spoken word.

Todd has been a professional educator for the past 15 years. He is currently the principal of an alternative learning center in central Arkansas.

Todd uses poetry in almost every aspect of life to inspire. He uses mnemonic devices when coaching youth sports and perceptive prose to advise colleagues and friends. He is poetic, in some way, even when dealing with society's complications.

The piece, "My People—My Sins—My Triumph" is an example of how his passion for the best solution, which may not always be the popular solution, resonates. Todd will be launching a website for student-behavior-management products in 2015.

Authors Note: I use multiple methods to ignite my writing. One of those methods includes beginning with a lingering concept, which leads to freestyle writing. It may take several revisions to reach the desired creation. The poem "Just Breathe" is one piece that speaks to this process.

The concept began as a tribute to dating someone different from your usual dates when you least expect it. However, just as unexpected, you realize this person's behavior motivates you to stay in your comfort zone.

Contact: parkereducator@gmail.com

Katerria "Starr" Doty

Katerria "Starr" Doty was born in 1977 in Chicago where she currently resides. She graduated from Olive Harvey College with an associate's degree in early childhood education. She runs a home child care, which she founded in 2004.

Katerria is the happy mother of two daughters: Timerria and WinterStarr Daniel. It was difficult to write while dealing with the loss of her best friend Kizzy. She said, "Trying to focus through the tears and the pain of a broken heart was paralyzing." As you read her pieces, know that she pushed hard to deliver them.

Author's Note: I freely admit that when I wrote "Reconnection To Reality," it was healing for me. I began another stage of the grieving process and started relating to life again after losing my best friend and soul mate. The tears continued, so I allowed them to flow, I felt all the pent up anger and resistance fading from my core. I began to reflect on other relationships in my life.

Dad I often think about you and I now understand, that your experiences have made you disappointed with women. You couldn't be what I wanted and needed you to be—a protector, provider, and nurturer! I realize that my Creator protected me by keeping you absent. Your presence may not have been what was best for me at the time, but I'm grateful.

These eyes and feet of mine, everything about them—are you R.W., and I thank you for them. I can't deny the great attributes from your bloodline. Your children have all grown up, and you have proven yourself as a super grandad to all your grandchildren! To God be the glory! Greater things are in store.

Your grateful daughter, Starr

Mom, I love you. I thank God for you! I lift you up, for you are our Queen! We can't bring back yesteryear; however, we have today. Now I understand your upbringing and the things that were against you. Mom, you sacrificed so much to be different from your mom and to give us what you lacked, which is what good parents do. We, your children, thank you for all you've given us. We love you and celebrate the woman you are. Your many sacrifices are appreciated!

Your loving daughter,

~Katerria Son'ta Doty

Pamela S.B. Fagen

Pamela S.B. Fagen considers herself as a modern-day foodie, registered and licensed dietitian/nutritionist, writer, teacher, administrator, and analyst. Pamela has a bachelor's degree in home economics/dietetics and a master's degree in human services administration. She is a member of many social and civic organizations.

Pamela has learned through experience and study to try to find a philosophical principle in every life experience. Pamela is not a stranger to writing and the power of the written and spoken word. Much of her writing style illustrates her spiritual connections. She is passionate about seeking understanding, desiring to be understood, and communicating these concepts.

She says, learning to write is a healing process. She contributes it to experiencing life's pain and pleasure for many years while struggling to get through a difficult transitional seasons in her life. At that time, she found another part of herself that was hidden and never before expressed. Each day during that difficult season, she rushed home to fill pads with experiences that seemed to pour out like an overflowing well. That was when she began healing with each journal entry.

Author's Note: It is with great pleasure that I share some insight with you on many subjects. Exploring our themes from "I cried Last night" to having a "Love Jones" not only made me think about "bittersweet" aspects of life but also how to "set myself free" from anything that makes me feel bound.

It was great working with our personal writing group. We have fond memories, and you will read about them in our chapter dedicated to Kizzy, the POP writer who departed.

This has been a rewarding experience for me and one that I am thankful for and will forever cherish. I hope you enjoy Free Admission.

Jor'Danna

Jor'Danna Davis believes that expressing one's self is therapy to the soul. She is no stranger to adversity and chronicles parts of her personal journey and her inner thoughts in her writing. Through her pieces, she hopes to entertain, inspire, and relate to her readers.

A native of Chicago, Jor'Danna graduated with a bachelor's degree from Grambling State University and master's degrees from Roosevelt University and Lewis University. She has worked in the field of education for several years. Jor'Danna has a passion for youth education and mental health, especially in the African American community.

Author's Notes

Jor'Danna leads the book off with 'Clutter Free" In this piece she rids herself of a past that haunted her for years. Jor'Danna also freed herself from the hair war. Check out "Mahogany Crown." She truly believe you can free yourself from what ever holds you back.

Kenya Renee

Kenya Renee, high school educator/philanthropist/writer/producer/actress, has developed an array of stage productions, produced independent films, held fund raising events, and created platforms for small business owners and fellow artists to showcase their talents and ideas.

After being exhausted with viewing films and theatrical plays that lacked substance, she put the pen to the pad and wrote the hit stage play "The Cycle," which toured five cities before its closing performance in Chicago, IL. Kenya has also implemented a complete array of entertainment instruments, which act as confidence builders, through her entertainment company, FAM Entertainment Theater Company NFP. The company focuses on achievement and motivation through entertainment.

Kenya Renee believes that hands-on expression combined with poetry and music inspires insight for community growth. She embraces speaking engagements at corporate events, convention exhibitions, peer group gatherings, women's outings, and school-sponsored events. Her next project is a debut film titled "Deacon's Choice," which is a powerful story of an ex-Chicago politician who embodies the trickle effect of selfishness, cover-ups, addiction, and consequence.

Kenya is delighted to have completed this beautiful expression and wishes that all who read this book, especially her entire family and friends, will become inspired.

Author's Notes: The cost of celebrity. Check out this chapter, and ask yourself at what cost? I encourage you to acknowledge your most bittersweet moment. Read "A Missed Moment" it will ignite you, I truly believe that a dream is reality in the making.

Contact: www.facebook.com/kenyatheproducer

Sharon Payne

Sharon Payne was born on the westside of Chicago on July 14, 1965. After moving to the suburbs, she met a teacher, Mrs. Walters, who encouraged her to read and write at an early age. By the fifth grade, she realized that she had a gift and was encouraged by her older cousin, Maenolia, to write poetry. It became a hobby that she loved.

Sharon graduated from East Aurora High School and attended Waubonsee Community College in Sugar Grove, IL, where she studied child development, secretarial science, and computer science. She has held positions at Nicor Gas, Todd School, Cowherd Middle School, and West Aurora High School. Sharon has also been a director at Kinder-Care and the Grand Boulevard Center for after-school and summer programs.

She is now living in Naperville, IL and has two adult children—Timothy and Jasmine—whom she adores as well as two grandchildren. She is now working on her next set of poetry and short stories.

Sharon would like to thank her family, friends, and a special someone who took the time to listen to her, encourage her, critique her, and edge her on when she felt like giving up on this project because of deaths, sickness, and just life in general.

Author's Note: This project brought complete strangers together and we opened our hearts to each other as well as you, the reader. Some of my favorite pieces are "No Time," "The Neighborhood Bully," and "My Curves." I hope you enjoy reading them as much as I enjoyed writing them.

Contact: shabuwitu@yahoo.com

Adrienne Bruce created Pen On Paper (POP) Writers 'Guild for the purpose of gathering groups of individuals who are like-minded and have a passion for expressing themselves through a variety of writing styles.

POP was also formed to birth new ideas and stimulates gifted writers to push out their thoughts and share their inner feelings with readers through a plethora of publications.

Native Chicagoan Adrienne Bruce's artistic talent is generational. Her father, a window designer for several State Street department stores, also painted viaducts in the Hyde Park neighborhood; while her artsy-crafty mother taught her how to loom, crochet, sew, and cook. She freely gives credit where credit is due, recognizing that she inherited her parents' artistic overflow. She considers herself doubly blessed.

Adrienne Bruce is a former cosmetology teacher for Chicago Public Schools. She enjoys teaching in an industry that promotes education, fashion, and design. Whether she is styling hair, painting a landscape, designing a piece of jewelry, or writing poetry, beauty is the end result, and it is beauty that intrigues others, which in turn brings her great joy.

Mrs. Adrienne Bruce says, "Creating with your hands goes back to the beginning of time. God created the heavens and the earth as well as man. He formed and fashioned life. God gave us the ability to create beautiful things with our hands. People today don't take advantage of their God-given talents or even try to discover the gifts that lie within. These historical customs should be embraced, regenerated, and retrieved to enhance our natural talents of today."

Beautiful Blessings is Mrs. Bruce's jewelry design company, she says, she believes hers are, "Designs That Demand A Second Look."

Contact: www.beautifulblessings2u.com
Facebook : AdriennebeautifulblessingsBruce

Valerie Winkfield
Paper Artist

Valerie "Val" Winkfield is a native of Chicago and loves the city. Valerie grew up on the south side, attended Park Manor elementary school and graduated from Hirsch High School. She went on to Fisk University in Nashville, TN. It was there that she discovered her love for arts and crafts. Val only raised two sons but came from a large family of seven sisters and three brothers. She always found time to be creative, whether it was sewing, drawing or cutting paper collages.

Val admits that after retiring from Northwestern Hospital as a pharmaceutical technician for 38 years, her life as an artist began. She loves to cruise the tropical islands every chance she gets. Taking much needed vacations gives her inspiration when she is in a creative mode. Since retiring, she has time to design beautiful, exquisite, frameable greeting cards. These cards are on display at many outdoor festivals. People are amazed at the intricate details she puts into every greeting card. Her pieces are fabulous works of art.

Val was honored to illustrate for this publication. She says, "Just think, at one time this was only a hobby, but now it's a business that I didn't see coming. Thank you, POP Writers Guild for giving me the opportunity to share my paper passion with the world."

Contact: Valspaperpassion@yahoo.com

*All inserted artwork is in black and white. To see the images in color, visit: Val's Paper Passion on Facebook.

J.D. Cooper
Editor and Publisher

J.D Cooper is the publisher for the POP Writers Guild. She has an intensity for editing and provides the layout and the designs for the interiors of books. She is the owner of Jazzi CreationsPublishing Service, located in Chicago, IL

J.D. is a gifted author who has written various poetry books and self-publishing guides. She is the originator of the Birth That Book Workshops $_{TM}$ for adults and youth. She has a love for reading and writing Christian Fiction

She has encouraged several to follow their dream to write and publish their books of all genres. Those who enter her workshop with an urge to write or publish a book are nurtured to release to their fullest potential. She gives the courage to PUSH (proceed until satisfaction happens), and that precisely is what will occur without a struggle.

J.D's first loves are poetry, creative writing, and journalism. She holds degrees in the Literary Arts, and Psychology.

She is a Certified Addictions Counselor. Her extraordinary imagination is a benefit when she uses it to connect these professions concurrently to produce exciting poetry and short stories. She also uses the creative flow in editing, publishing and to lead powerfully effective writing groups. She has a spirit of excellence and creates products that are polished, professional, and innovative. POP Writers' Guild welcomed her as a valuable asset.

Contact: www.jazzicreations.com

JamieLynn Warber
Graphic Designer

JamieLynn Warber, artist, writer, graphic designer, photographer, and Mother. Once again, brings her dramatic style of art and design to another anthology book as the highlighted graphic designer for the POP Writer's Guild Art Gallery. On the pages of this edition, several selections of her work can be found. JamieLynn amazed us with her phenomenal artistic design ability when she presented her one of kind masterful art piece for the cover of a previous publication. *Layers of Life* made its debut in 2014.

She took to writing and art at an early age. During her freshman year of high school, she fell in love with a design school in Schaumburg, IL, finishing there with a bachelor's degree in fine arts and graphic design.

JamieLynn puts all aspects of art in her life as a way to express herself. Although she is an extraordinary artist, she has discovered how to use Photoshop in a way that allows her freedom from the clean up of chalk, paint, or airbrush. She pulls her inspiration from everywhere and has an incredible respect for art. She treats each piece as though they are real human beings living their lives after the dry pages end. JamieLynn says, "I want to write nearly every experience, each tantalizing thought. No one will ever know the passion, the high, I get from things overlooked." She likes to think that she brings a unique view to the world that gives those who experience her work a bit of inspiration.

She says, "I believe that without being fully self-expressive and imaginative, there is no life."

*All inserted artwork is in black and white. To see the images in color,
visit: jamielynn-gabrichwarber.fineartamerica.com

FREE ADMISSION

140704130208

Access To The Soul

140704130208

P.O.P GALLERY

FEATURING JAMIELYNN WARBER

Fancy Flight - Black

Fancy Flight - white

Willow Curve

Embrace

Curious Fairy - white

Embrace

Compelling

Alien Flower

Absent Fairy

Topiary

Featured art for sale at www.fineartamerica.com

Mission

The P.O.P. Writers Guild was created for the purpose of gathering groups of individuals who are like-minded and who have a passion to express themselves through a variety of writing styles.

P.O.P. was also formed to birth new ideas and stimulate gifted writers to push out their thoughts and share their inner feelings with potential readers through a plethora of publications.

"Don't be a writer, be writing.

- William Faulkner

Our History

The P.O.P. Writers Guild is the brainchild of Adrienne Bruce, and was created for the purpose of gathering groups of individuals who are like-minded and who have a passion to express themselves through a variety of writing styles.

Established in February of 2012, the P.O.P. Writers Guild exists to birth new ideas and to stimulate gifted writers to push forth their thoughts and share their inner feelings with potential readers through a plethora of publications.

In August 2012, we released our first compilation, *Don't Get It Twisted*, a beautiful work consisting of the poetry and short story works from our "FIRST OFFICIAL CHAPTER" of P.O.P. writers members.

Consisting of at least eight (8) writers per group, members of the P.O.P. Writers Guild meet once a month and have bi-weekly teleconference calls to motivate writers to create and stay on course. Our meetings consist of fun writing games and activities and reciting our created masterpieces, amongst other things.

Iron sharpens iron is our oath, and our responsibility is to listen attentively, critique objectively and to make positive suggestions.

As we collaborate, wonderful, heartfelt pieces are born and prepared to share with the world.

PLEASE SUPPORT THE P.O.P WRITER'S SPONSORSHIP PROGRAM.

2014 RECIPIENT

Please support Our 2014 recipient.
Send all donations to:
www.popwriters.com

Luverta Reams

Are you an aspiring English or Publishing Major who needs support while obtaining your Masters Level Degree?

If so we are looking for you.

I am aspiring to be a publisher and ultimately, own my own publishing company. I've had the chance to enhance my editing and software skills. I believe these are steps in the right direction and are crucial for my education. I believe that this degree at Pace University will expand my understanding of the industry. Not only will this program give the connections needed, but it will also give more of the practical application that is necessary to achieve my goals. I am excited to become a part of Pace University's community. I am expecting the academics and life experiences of this education to catapult me into greatness.

I will be leaving August 24, 2014. School begins September 3, 2014. I will be living on campus beginning in January 2015. My tuition cost is an estimated $42,000 with the expectant May 2016 graduation date.

We are accepting applications for our 2015 Scholarship Program starting March 1, 2015.
For more details,
please go to www.popwriters.com

You Could Be Next!

YOUR WEALTH IS MORE THAN JUST MONEY
LEAVE A LEGACY!

PUBLISH YOUR OWN BOOK

JAZZI CREATIONS SELF-PUBLISHING SERVICE, provides the professional assistance and preparation for book publishing

JAZZI CREATIONS, will guide you through a step by step self-publishing process and provide the resources necessary to bring your manuscript to a polished book that will make you proud.

JAZZI CREATIONS, is a unique company that produces transformational insight regarding those stories that you have dreamed about writing for years. Those stories are waiting for immediate release. Our main goal is to help bring the book that you have written to fruition.

By publishing your book through JAZZI CREATIONS, you are choosing an affordable and convenient way to achieve first-rate digital publication.

The Self Publishing process starts with your manuscript submission.

Even if you are not a writer we can ghostwrite your story. You will own and retain all rights to your project because we are here to provide a service. Once finished we turnover your book to you to sell and all the profits remain yours.

JAZZI CREATIONS SELF-PUBLISHING SERVICE
offers workshops
for youth and adults

Writing a book is not something that takes great talent—it takes great determination and will power.

For more information on this
wonderful opportunity
Email:publisher@jazzi.com
Or
Visit our website:
www.jazzicreations.com

Coming Soon!

P.O.P member contacts: 773 419 2443
Follow P.O.P Writers Guild on Facebook
E-mail: popwriters@gmail.com

www.ingramcontent.com/pod-product-compliance
Lightning Source LLC
Chambersburg PA
CBHW071917290426
44110CB00013B/1395